THE LAKE EFFECT

A Lake Michigan Mosaic

FRED CARLISLE

For
My dear Betts
A treasure forever

For my daughters
Lindy, Becky, Ginna Lee, and Jana
So admired and loved by me

And for Andrea Rutledge,
my stepdaughter,
in gratitude and love

The Lake Effect
© Copyright 2022, Fred Carlisle

Cover art: **Cascade** © 2022 Alexis Rockman / Artists Rights Society (ARS), New York

No part of this book may be reproduced, stored in a retrieval system, or transmitted in any form or by any means electronic, mechanical, photocopying, recording or otherwise, without the prior consent of the publisher.

For information or permission, contact:
Mission Point Press
2554 Chandler Road
Traverse City, Michigan 49696
www.MissionPointPress.com

Design by Sarah Meiers

Printed in the United States of America

ISBN: 978-1-958363-18-8
Library of Congress Control Number: 2022912987

*"Water, the greatest of desires,
is the truly inexhaustible, divine gift."*
Gaston Bachelard

*"We commonly do not remember that it is, after all,
always the first person that is speaking."*
Henry David Thoreau, *Walden*

CONTENTS

Lake Michigan	fmviii
Reading *The Lake Effect*	fmix

- 1 • ORIGINS: **Ogden Dunes and the Beach** — 1
- 2 • ORIGINS: **The Lucas Home in Gary, Indiana** — 9
- 3 • **Water 1** — 23
- 4 • **Rediscovering Lake Michigan** — 25
- 5 • **Lake Michigan Rising** — 31
- 6 • **Water 2: Words and Images** — 43
- 7 • **The Invasive Juggernaut** — 52
- 8 • **Water 3** — 58
- 9 • **The Return** — 60
- 10 • **The Lake Effect** — 66
- 11 • **Water 4** — 70
- 12 • **The Gold Coast: Tourism, Affluence, and the Others** — 76
- 13 • **Water 5** — 102
- 14 • **The Force of the Lake** — 107
- 15 • **Leaving Lake Michigan** — 111

Acknowledgments	113
Notes and Sources	112
Sources for Topics	120

Lake Michigan map

Reading *The Lake Effect*

I stood ankle deep in Lake Michigan for the first time when I was two years old. My fascination with the lake began then and has continued throughout my life. The lake has been a constant presence for me no matter where I've been—near the lake or far from it.

I am still deeply moved by the lake's mesmerizing beauty. I've been impressed by the way it sustains the economies and societies of every place along its shores. I understand the extensive water culture it has enabled. I have learned how human intervention and carelessness have polluted, damaged, and degraded it. I know its power to drown swimmers, wreck ships, destroy beaches, and consume houses. I know the magnificent beauty and the danger and destructiveness of snow and ice. I am fascinated by this complex mosaic of the Great Lake.

The Lake Effect: A Lake Michigan Mosaic flows through my personal experiences and reflection—moving from myself to wider perspectives and themes that include the aesthetic, psychic, historic, economic, social, and cultural effects of the lake, and of water generally. I treat such analytical abstractions as inseparably intertwined in our lives. We live them *in situ*. In this sense, the experiential gives meaning to the conceptual as the conceptual interprets the experiential. I am trying to portray, in part, e.g., the experiencing of the economy and of the water culture of the lake.

The book explores as well the functions and power of water broadly. On the one hand, it is magic in the Herman Melville sense: "All around the town stand thousands upon thousands of mortal men fixed on ocean reveries . . . They must get as nigh water as they possibly can . . . There is magic in it" (*Moby Dick*, 796). There is even scientific evidence that "being by water makes us healthier, happier, reduces stress, and brings us peace" (Nichols, 11). We might even be hardwired for what Wallace Nichols names "Blue Mind." On the other hand, water can also be the "adversary" Gaston Bachelard describes in "Violent Water." *The Lake Effect* speaks also of fierce storms, damaging winter ice, shipwrecks—perhaps the black magic of water.

Bachelard also writes, "Water, the greatest of desires, is the truly inexhaustible, divine gift. I cannot sit beside a stream without falling into a profound reverie" (176). That balance—water as comfort and water as threat—is what I'm trying to capture.

At several points, I address the problem of trying to write both the romance and reality. We do find ways to enjoy life's beauty and pleasure. How could we stand it otherwise? We must also recognize its bleak, harsh, painful realities. So how do we write it differently? How do I express both the romance of the lake and its realities—alternatively, ironically, discontinuously? In "The Story of a Day," Louise Glück expresses the dilemma beautifully:

"I was torn between a structure of oppositions/and a narrative structure—"

Instead of being a continuous narrative with clear continuity, *The Lake Effect* consists of a series of different moments, discoveries, stories, and histories. It is episodic and oppositional—in Glück's sense. That is, it gathers a series of pieces that might seem disparate or discontinuous but that emotionally and experientially are fluid and continuous. They are whole or consistent in me, and, I am hopeful, in you as well. They are part of the complex Lake Michigan mosaic—part of the flow of the lake and the fluidity of the natural and human worlds.

• 1 •

ORIGINS
Ogden Dunes and the Beach

"Images of our earliest imagination govern our entire life."
Gaston Bachelard

US 12 followed the New York Central tracks from Gary to Ogden Dunes and Lake Michigan. We drove there several times every summer until World War II interrupted visits with my grandparents. It was only fifteen miles from their house to the beach, but to a youngster it seemed to take forever—especially on those hot days when the car overheated, forcing my father to pull off the road and wait until it cooled.

As a distraction, we'd look for the Twentieth Century Limited—the express streamliner drawing passenger cars and Pullmans toward New York City, a mysterious and worldly place, the city Grand Central Station described every week on the radio as "the crossroads of a million private lives, a gigantic stage on which are played a thousand dramas daily." I don't recall how often we saw the train, but we watched for it every time. Even on the hottest summer days, it was exciting—maybe the exotic Limited, definitely the beach.

We turned left off the highway, crossed the railroad tracks, passed by a small guardhouse, then followed a winding cinder road toward the lake. My impatience grew with every turn. But finally, we would arrive.

The hot sand burned my feet as I crossed the dune toward the lake. The sharp dune grass slashed at my ankles. The glare made me squint. I carried a towel, maybe a few other things. My parents, uncles, aunts, and cousins carried umbrellas and picnic baskets. A few steps further—I could feel the cool air from the lake. Then we were there.

Only a few photographs remain. The first—two-year-old Freddie ankle deep in the water and pointing at something just to the right of the photographer—was taken July 23, 1937. Other pictures show my parents, cousins, aunts, uncles, and me, digging in the sand, wading in the shallows, and lying or sitting under a large beach umbrella. There are no chairs. I see blankets, towels, toy shovels and buckets, a beach ball, a thermos, but no picnic baskets, after all. They may be

Freddie, age two, Ogden Dunes

in another photo, or simply in my imagination. The beach—there must be a picnic basket. My mother wears a white bathing cap and one-piece bathing suit. My father wears trunks in some photographs, in others, a swimsuit with shoulder straps. My grandfather appears in one picture—a surprise. I'd forgotten he sometimes went with us. I don't remember my grandmother ever going.

I am two and five in these photographs. I remember being there—although the photos doubtless have sharpened my memory. I do recall playing at the water's edge—pushing through waist-deep water to a sandbar just offshore. I recall waves so high, water so roiled and brown, my cousins and I were not allowed in. On those days, we wore jackets or shirts. But the pictures show us at the beach on calm, sunny days. The water is flat. The horizon line distinct. The sky cloudless—except for distant cumulus clouds in one photo. They form a backdrop to the few houses scattered along the top of the front dune. On clear days, we could see Chicago miles away along the southwest shore of the lake.

...

There is a wholeness for me about those early years—grandparents, home, the beach, Chicago, and the lake. Every aspect is inseparably intertwined with every other. Experience is dense and complex no matter how we try to simplify it. This intertwining—the wholeness of my experience—is the origin of *The Lake Effect*.

Primal, childhood experiences transformed Lake Michigan into a place of lifelong desire—a magical, mystical lake—a place of longing and power so deeply embedded in my heart and soul that decades of experience and knowledge about the lake have left unchanged. I understand the irony. I've been captured by the magic of the lake and its mythical purity. I have also learned how polluted it was then and how invaded it has become by non-native sea life. Lake Michigan, even in my childhood, was suffering from industrial, municipal, and agricultural runoff. Some parts of the lake were even dying from lack of oxygen. We adjust, however, and the romance sweeps us away.

4 Origins

• • •

For me then, Ogden Dunes was simply a winding road, the blowout depression of my grandparents' vacant lot, dune grass, stunted beech trees, the beach itself, and the lake that seemed so clear and pure. Ogden Dunes, however, was much more than a child could know or care about. It had been incorporated as a town in 1925 by twenty landowners who sought a right-of-way across the New York Central tracks. After a lengthy approval process, the town constructed a new road and entrance. At that point, Ogden Dunes Realty began advertising the community as a "highly restricted residential suburb" (*Ogden Dunes*, 31). It was not far from Gary, then a thriving steel city, and close enough to Chicago to attract University of Chicago faculty and staff as residents.

By 1939, there were 132 summer and year-round houses. Forty-three families lived there full time. It had become a serious, if very small, town. The realty company published a periodic town newsletter, *The Sandpiper*. Community women organized a Woman's Club. Mail was being delivered. Twenty-one residents attended a nearby Portage County school.

Residents were drawn to the dunes and the lake, I assume, by the same longing I've felt—a desire that may be universal. I like Herman Melville's way of saying it: "Right and left the streets take you waterward . . . All around the town stand thousands upon thousands of mortal men fixed on ocean reveries . . . Here come more crowds, pacing straight for the water . . . They must get as nigh water as they possibly can . . . There is magic in it" (*Moby Dick*, 795, 796). And, we also know from Ahab's quest, there is danger and death in it, as well.

• • •

In the 1920s, the South Shore Railroad Line initiated a four-year poster project that captured some of that magic and appealed to the longing. Commercial poster art in Chicago had a long and impressive history. There was also a vibrant printing industry there, so talented illustrators and expert printers produced a distinguished series. The artists designed brightly colored images that created a romantic vision of the Indiana dunes. The posters promoted the railroad, to be sure. The South Shore Line's offering of "fast trains operated electrically from Chicago to South Bend, Indiana," or a similar service, appeared on each one. The posters also inspired Chicagoans to visit the dunes and even live there—to buy and build, for example, in the town of Ogden Dunes.

Known formally as the Chicago South Shore and South Bend Railroad, the South Shore initiated service in 1901. The Lake Shore Line, as it was first named, persisted into the 1920s, but it was struggling financially. After Samuel Insull purchased it in 1925, he renamed and transformed the South Shore into a highly successful, award-winning interurban line. By the late 1920s, its ridership exceeded three million passengers annually, and its revenues had increased dramatically. It reached its peak in 1929. During the Depression, unsurprisingly, passengers and revenue declined precipitously. The railroad cut back staff and trains and eliminated dining and parlor cars. The South Shore, however, did survive. We were riding the orange cars in the late 1940s. Since then, it has persisted through good and bad times. It is one of the few interurban trains still operating in the U.S. It runs trains over the route established early in the 20th century.

Of all the posters created, only thirty eight survived—twenty three of them depict lake, beach, or dune scenes. I bought reproductions of four from the Chicago Historical Society in 2002. "The Dunes Beaches" poster shows a bright-eyed, smiling young flapper girl, wearing a black bathing costume, headscarf, black mid-calf stockings, and beach shoes. She is sitting under a beach umbrella brilliantly colored in red, orange, yellow, and green. She is gazing at me, as if to say, "Come join me at the beach. You'll love Lake Michigan." Behind her in more muted colors, I see the lake and figures sitting and lying on the sand.

"Come join me at the beach." *(Courtesy of Chicago History Museum)*

"Moonlight in Duneland," the cover image for the illustrated history of the railroad, portrays a summer scene—a full, yellow moon is descending between two large trees; two figures are seated near their campfire at the lake's edge. It is a quiet and peaceful moment.

The vibrant "Spring in the Dunes" pictures a cluster of white and amber blossoms rising from dark green leaves in the foreground, then a band of chartreuse grass or sand dotted with white, yellow, and violet blooms, tall vermilion trees in the background, and in the distance, dunes silhouetted in blue-gray beneath a light gray sky. It is representational but hardly literal—yet wonderfully appealing in its radiance.

The posters feature fall and winter scenes, as well as spring and summer. There are pictures of skiing and tobogganing down the dunes, even a poster showing the ski jump at Ogden Dunes that hosted international competitions. It lasted, however, only four years, and closed before my birth. A few posters represent the steel industry. Two, no surprise, advertise Notre Dame football. The South Shore did after all serve South Bend from Chicago. It ran football specials from Chicago during the season.

Altogether, the posters speak to life in the area and celebrate year-round opportunity and activity at the Indiana Dunes. They center on the dunes, the lake, seasonal activity, and implicitly on residential development. They focused the longing for lakeshore or seaside on a specific place. Who wouldn't want to live there—if one could?

• • •

Were I to return to Ogden Dunes now, I'd drive on paved streets into a town of roughly six hundred homes and 1,200 residents. The Ogden Dunes Town Council governs the community. A police force and a volunteer fire department provide security. The town has established a community fund and a historical society. There are various clubs residents may join—book, bridge, garden, Lions. Housing development has virtually saturated the town's 1.5 square miles. Homes often sell for $400,000-500,000, a few for close to $1 million. Lots can be listed for as much as $150,000. The town typifies the decades of development all along the Lake Michigan shore. The lake's "distinctive natural features are more pronounced outside the [lake] basin, however; inside, they have been all but obliterated by urbanization. Close to Lake Michigan less than 1 percent of the natural habitat is still intact" (Grady, 18). It is a dramatically different world from what I first knew.

Were I to walk along the beach now, instead of a few scattered houses, I'd see large, carefully landscaped homes, some with lawns, lining the top of the front dune, and a similar row on the other side of Lake Shore Drive. There are no available lots here. I would also walk beside a lake the town monitors regularly for water quality. It posts green, yellow, and red notices to inform swimmers. Yellow warns children and the elderly that water quality may be compromised. Red tells people the water exceeds EPA standards for E. coli. Swimming is prohibited. I would also be walking beside a lake that over time has been invaded by predatory and non-native species that have attacked and even wiped out some native lake life and disrupted its fisheries. And in recent years I would see as well a severely eroded beach and houses threatened by high water.

In spite of these facts about pollution, the destructive fish and organisms that have invaded the lake, and high water levels, Lake Michigan still captivates us by its expanse and beauty. We can't escape the romance. We cannot overcome our deep desire for beach and lake—for water. "There is magic in it" (*Moby Dick*, 796).

• 2 •

ORIGINS
The Lucas Home in Gary, Indiana

"America's Magic Industrial City" on the lake

My Lucas grandparents lived at 536 Polk Street in Gary, Indiana, on a block of single-family homes built close together. Only a narrow, paved walkway from front to back separated them from their neighbor's house. When the side windows were open, you could hear voices almost as if you were inside the other house. I remember people talking or shouting—sometimes we heard music—but I don't recall anything specific. Normally, people closed the windows and drew down the blinds—except in the heat of summer.

Born in Milltown, New Brunswick, in 1882, my grandfather was the fourth of eleven children. His father, Reverend Aquila Lucas, emigrated from England to Canada to serve the Methodist Society of the New World. He was assigned first to Prince Edward Island, where he met and married my grandfather's mother, Harriet Bridges, in 1875. Over time, Aquila moved from one circuit to another in the Canadian Maritimes. Late in his career he devoted himself to International Sunday School and traveled to the Caribbean and the Americas. At some point, the family moved to London, Ontario, where my grandfather, Robert Bridges Lucas, grew up.

Born in Toronto in 1880, my grandmother grew up there as Isabel Henry. They were married in Toronto in 1907. By then, my grandfather had emigrated to the U.S. to work in the steel industry in Buffalo, New York, where my mother was born in 1910. The family moved to Gary in 1911 for my grandfather's work at the new U.S. Steel plant.

We visited them in Gary every summer until World War II, once during the war (my father had saved enough gas-rationing coupons), and then most summers after the war, until 1953, when they moved to Clearwater, Florida, after my grandfather's retirement in 1947. My father typically combined our post-war summer trips with business at the Equitable Life Insurance Company in Chicago. We spent most Christmases in Gary as well, until the late 1940s, when my parents decided we should enjoy Christmas at home. I am guessing, also, that my father's patience with his domineering in-laws had probably run its course. In summertime, we could at least escape to the beach and to Cubs or White Sox baseball in Chicago.

. . .

There was a small front yard at 536 that my grandfather watered every summer evening after dinner. He unwound his garden hose, turned the nozzle to a light spray, and then slowly moved the flow back and forth, soaking the grass thoroughly. I sat on the wooden front steps or stood beside him watching his nightly ritual and imagining the scent of Lake Michigan in that fine spray. Directly on the lake, Gary drew its water from there then, as well as now. Although I asked over and over, he never let me hold the hose, even for a minute. It must have been his Zen time.

My grandmother's flower gardens bordered the even smaller backyard. I imagine a profusion of daffodils, irises, tulips, peonies, daisies, even a few daylilies, and against the back of the house, a lilac bush. She cared for her flowers as carefully as my grandfather tended the grass. Just past the garden at the back of the lot, their two-car garage opened onto a paved alley. Inside the garage smelled of old wood, oil, gasoline, and automobile.

A set of wide wooden stairs led into a glass-enclosed front porch—a pleasant, extra room in summer, but just an unheated and cold space in winter. The real front door opened into a wide living room that extended from one side of the house to the other. Just to the left sat my grandfather's chair, with a circular ash tray stand next to it that held his pipes, pipe rack, and tobacco. A glass-doored bookcase stood against the wall behind his chair. The books he was reading were on a nearby table. At the end of a day, he would sit

Fred's grandparents, Robert and Isabel Lucas

smoking his pipe and reading the *Chicago Tribune*. In the evening, he also read books about the Great Lakes, especially *The American Lakes Series*, with a volume on each lake, published by Bobbs-Merrill in the 1940s.

He doubtless read all five volumes, but I can imagine his special interest in "Duneland," the chapter in *Lake Michigan* about the area where he and my grandmother owned a lot. It begins rhapsodically: "Wind and wave have conspired for ages past to create the dunes which border the southern and eastern coasts of Lake Michigan . . . Here at the front door of America's second city the forces of nature have created a strangely beautiful world, endowed with a wealth of floral and faunal life. Visitors from across the ocean who toured America a century ago were aroused to a state of ecstasy by the wild beauty of the dunes" (Quaife, 303).

That ideal world, however, was under attack. "In recent decades, the vast industrial development which centers at Chicago has pushed steadily eastward around the lake shore, overwhelming Duneland as it advances with a congeries of cities whose roaring furnaces and bellowing smokestacks redden the sky by night and blacken it by day." The climax for the author is Gary, Indiana, and the Gary Works of U.S. Steel and its thousands of acres along the lake where "hills of sand were cut down and intervening marshes were filled . . . As industry advances, primitive life and beauty disappear" (Quaife, 310-311). It was a classic conflict between a capitalist economic motive and the aesthetics of natural beauty.

The author saw this in the 1940s, long before the dramatic commercial and residential developments of subsequent decades, the poisoning of lake waters, and the introduction of non-native fish and organisms—the destructive effects of human intervention.

U.S. Steel purchased eight thousand acres extending seven miles along the lakeshore and two miles inland. On that site it constructed a 3,500-acre plant for twelve blast furnaces, almost one hundred open-hearth furnaces, and four rolling mills. The city of Gary seemed to arise almost overnight. "I see a city rise as if by magic, in proportions vast and splendid," said the Indiana governor in 1907

(Davich, 23). Reading that reminded me of my time in Dubai during its architectural boom. We'd drive by a place and ask, "Was that building there last week?" An exaggeration indeed, but expressive. U.S. Steel asked the Gary Land Company to design and build the city. The company built houses for management and skilled workers and sold lots to others. It was also charged with developing an infrastructure that would serve two hundred thousand residents. Gary became a model city with a school system that set an example nationally for innovation. It wasn't long before it became one of the largest cities in the state.

I have no idea how my grandfather felt about the desolation of the south shore. He was a mill superintendent for U.S. Steel and a property owner in Duneland. He read about the lakes. My grandparents displayed handsome Louise Wilder oil paintings of the dunes and Lake Michigan. They obviously valued the lake for its beauty and pleasure, as well as for its commercial and industrial uses. He might simply have compartmentalized the two realities or simply been satisfied with modern industry and happy with what was left of the dunes.

A few years ago, at a Charlottesville bookstore, I happened upon a first edition of *Lake Michigan* from the Bobbs-Merrill series. That discovery took me back to what I'm writing about here—my grandparents, Gary, Ogden Dunes, and Lake Michigan. Although he read the book seventy five years ago, I began to wonder what might have interested him in the book I'm holding in my hand. What did he learn that might connect with my memories, experience, and reflection? That book, published in 1944, will turn up from time to time as we go along—as my grandfather will.

In the living room beyond his chair, a secretary-style desk stood on the far left wall, a cabinet radio next to it. During our summer visits, we listened to WGN and Bob Elson broadcasting White Sox games from Comiskey Park, or Jack Brickhouse doing Cubs games from Wrigley Field. A large oriental rug covered most of the living room floor. There might have been a piano at the near end of the room. But I've lost that to time, as well as the arrangement of other furniture.

Family Christmases at the Lucas's were a real treat. My grandparents placed the tree near the windows at the front of the house. On Christmas morning, presents from Santa and from family and relatives were spread under the tree. My cousin Bob Martin's family was always there, and my mother's brother, Bob, sometimes brought his family from northern Michigan. We filled the house—four Carlisles, five Martins, five in Bob Lucas's family, and my grandparents.

Granddad and Nanna imposed strict rules on Christmas morning. The adults escorted the children down the stairs blindfolded, so we couldn't see the tree and gifts across the living room. At the bottom of the stairs, they steered us into the kitchen where we ate a required full breakfast. Then, and only then, could we open presents.

My father's eight-millimeter color movies reinforce and give color to my memory—and doubtless help create it. They show the lighted tree, the gifts, the family sitting around the room—my sister crawling across the carpet, me in a cowboy suit—image after image.

I liked the morning better than the rest of the day. At the holiday dinner, my grandparents enforced still more rules. Sit up straight, chew your food, don't wash it down, wait until you've eaten to drink anything, don't talk much, and so on. I vaguely remember the family sitting around the table, but I don't remember the meal served nearly so well as I do the Thanksgiving dinners at my Carlisle grandparents', where they served turkey, two kinds of dressing, mashed white potatoes, yams, buttered noodles, green vegetables, and pumpkin pie with whipped cream. I do recall, however, the adults urging the kids to sample the dinner wine—and then smiling at our reaction. Who could stand that sharp and bitter stuff?

I don't know how my mother felt about the rules—after all, she grew up there—but the interference of his in-laws guiding and disciplining his children must have troubled my father. He set expectations for my sister and me, but warmly, fluidly, and lovingly. It was hard to escape Lucas-world in December—no beach or baseball in Chicago, just the Tivoli movie theater around the corner on 5th Avenue.

Grandfather Lucas was not unpleasant, just not especially warm and attentive. My grandmother seemed rather severe at times. She doubtless smiled more than I recall, but in my mind she rarely did. Many years later, after my grandfather had died in 1953, she moved to an apartment on North Washington Street in Delaware, Ohio, (my hometown) to be near my mother. Nanna then seemed sad and defeated—afraid to go to sleep at night for fear she would not wake up.

...

Every summer we visited Gary, my father and I would take the South Shore Railroad to Chicago for Cubs and White Sox baseball games. Granddad Lucas drove us to the station, where we boarded the bright orange, electrically powered train and headed for the baseball parks. The cars pulled quietly away from the station—no loud blasts of steam, no steel wheels spinning on the tracks as the locomotive accelerated and slowly gained traction—only the faint rumble of the wheels on the iron rails. We didn't talk much. The passing scene captivated me even though I was seeing the uglier parts of the towns we passed through—backyard trash heaps and garages with hollyhocks growing wild, warehouses, marginal businesses, occasionally a back garden. I couldn't see Lake Michigan from anywhere along the way, but we were riding on the South *Shore*—so it fit.

I recall stops in Hammond and East Chicago, and a few other places, before we arrived at the first Chicago station, Kensington at 115th Street. Then the orange cars moved on to 63rd, 53rd, Roosevelt Road, and Van Buren, ending at the Randolph Street terminal in the Chicago Loop—now known as the Millennium Station. There, we stepped off the train and looked for the stairway to the street. "It's this way, Freddie," my father said. We climbed the stairs and then looked for the Chicago "L."

We located a Red Line stop along State Street, climbed the metal stairs to the platform, and boarded a northbound train to Addison

Street, Wrigley Field, and the Cubbies, or a southbound "L" to the White Sox and Comiskey Park on West 35th.

We were riding the "L," let's say, to Wrigley Field in 1946. We got off at Addison Street and walked toward the stadium. "Hey, mister, how about a picture with your boy?" one photographer after another would ask. Or they simply snapped a picture and gave you a card with a number and an address—"Here you are. Send for them. It's only . . ." I have no idea what they cost. But there we are walking along a Chicago street to Wrigley—pictures of the two of us and closeups of me. My father is wearing a white dress shirt and tie. He's looking to his left toward the street. I'm focused on the camera. I'm eleven and wearing a collared, short-sleeve, white shirt. I'm frowning or squinting in each picture. It's a bright sunny day. My crew cut and cowlick are clear. There's a Monarch Beer sign behind me in one photo, and in one of my father and me, an "Olson"-something store is across the street.

• • •

The Cubs enjoyed a long fifteen-game home stand that July. They played the Reds, the Brooklyn Dodgers, the New York Giants, the Boston Braves, and the Phillies. We probably visited Gary in the middle of the month, so we could have seen the Dodgers, the Giants, or the Braves. The Cubs won five of those nine games. By the end of July, they were 52 and 43. I'm imagining that my father drank a beer or two at the game—maybe a local beer, Atlas or Prager (his favorite Schlitz if he could get it); we'd eat hot dogs; maybe shell peanuts; I probably had a Coke or a lemonade. We did what you do at the ballpark.

After the game, we retraced our steps to the "L," rode it back to the Randolph Street station, walked down the stairs to the track level, boarded the South Shore, and arrived in Gary about an hour later—just in time for dinner and my grandfather's evening water ritual.

• • •

Freddie and his father, Ervin Carlisle, walking to a Chicago baseball game.

In the summer of 1947, our grandparents took my cousin Bob and me to Canada to visit relatives. I was twelve, Bob, fourteen. My grandmother had badly sprained her ankle a few days before we left. She occupied the entire back seat—her leg extended across it for comfort. Bob and I alternated sitting by the door or in the middle of the front seat. We paid close attention to how long we sat in each position—no way one of us would get more time by the window than the other. Grandfather Lucas drove well enough, but occasionally he'd drop the right wheels off the edge of the road, then immediately pull back—nothing dangerous, other than the annoyed look my cousin gave him every time.

From Gary, we drove across southern Michigan and crossed to Windsor, Ontario, from Detroit. Even though the Great Lakes were not the focus of our trip, we did in effect circumnavigate Lakes Huron and Michigan, seeing the two only briefly, before we returned to Gary. I somehow sensed—or would like to think I did—the presence of the lakes all along the way. In fact, we were driving at every moment within the Great Lakes watershed. We were passing through places where land and lake affected one another.

We visited my grandfather's brothers, Harold and Albert Lucas, at the truck farm they owned and farmed near London. They grew crops in both open fields and greenhouses. They marketed their products at the London Produce Market. At the time we visited, Harold and Helen Gard were living together, unmarried. My grandmother visibly disapproved. I have no idea how she felt after they were in fact married in 1948.

During our visit to the Henrys in Toronto, one of the rides at a nearby amusement park made me sick. I vomited on the pavement and all over my shoes. Aunty Mart, a delightful, friendly, and witty woman, volunteered to clean them when we returned to their house. When I look closely at the formal photo of the six Henry sisters, Aunty Mart is the only one with a sparkle in her eyes and a slight smile.

From Toronto, we drove north in Ontario to North Bay, on the shore of Lake Nipissing, where Henry relatives lived. The city and lake are located as far north in Ontario as Sault Ste. Marie is in Michigan. The lake drains into Georgian Bay, the largest bay in the Great Lakes, bigger even than Lake Ontario.

I remember only two things about the North Bay visit: first, how shallow the lake was. We waded and waded and waded before the water came to our hips. Lake Nipissing is known for being unusually shallow everywhere. And second, the relatives asked about where Bob's and my heights came from. No one else in the family was so tall.

From North Bay, we headed west in Ontario toward the Sault and reentry into the U.S. As we passed Sudbury, my grandfather pointed out the exposed rock of the Canadian Shield. It's the largest mass of exposed Precambrian rock on Earth and covers much of northern and central Canada. I didn't understand at the time, but I do remember seeing it. The highway, still unpaved at several points, passed by Blind River, which later in life I knew as the small town near a lake where Ohio Wesleyan faculty and others from my hometown owned rather rudimentary summer cottages. Most had neither electricity nor bathrooms.

We crossed back into the U.S. at Sault Ste. Marie, passed the canal locks between Lake Superior and the lower lakes, and drove south in the Upper Peninsula to the straits of Mackinac, where we took the car ferry from the U.P. to Mackinaw City and northern Michigan. As we crossed, Lake Michigan opened on the right, to the west, and Lake Huron on the left and east. Mighty Mac, the five-mile suspension bridge across the straits, would not open for another ten years. From there we drove on south and then west into Indiana and to Gary.

I remember a few details so clearly, but I have no recollection, e.g., of the families' houses or of hotels or motels where we stayed, restaurants where we ate, or how and when I returned to Delaware. So many details have disappeared in the darkness of time. Nevertheless, the trip made a lifelong impression.

• • •

The Lucases lived in an urban residential neighborhood. We walked easily to several businesses up the street toward 5th Avenue—a small grocery and a drug store, I think, and an ice cream shop for sure. The ice cream came wrapped in cone shapes, which the server unwrapped and stuffed point first into a cone—no dipping necessary. It sat on the top of the cone, making it easier to spill, which I did at least once, on the sidewalk outside the shop. The Tivoli movie theater was located a few blocks away on 5th. I remember bank nights there, but none of the movies we might have seen. One Christmas Eve at my grandparents' church on 5th, a soprano sang a stunning Ave Maria.

The large brick building of Mercy Hospital stood a block away on Tyler Street—just beyond the hospital parking lot across from the house. We could see and hear hospital traffic at all times of the day and night—especially the flashing red lights and loud sirens of ambulances headed to the emergency room. For decades Mercy served as a premier healthcare facility for Gary, with a wide range of services and a school of nursing.

However mixed my feelings might be about my grandparents and 536 Polk Street, it was a home—my mother's home, the place where she grew up, went to school, left to attend college at Ohio Wesleyan in Delaware, the home where she and my father were married, and where we visited in tried-and-true family ways and enjoyed many things. My mother's parents raised her to be a good, kind, loving woman. And they raised a son, Robert Henry, who went on to a successful career in Great Lakes shipping. It was a home in a city neighborhood of middle-class families, most of whom lived in single-family houses. It was a stable and somewhat prosperous part of town. It was a good life for those years. And above all, my grandparents gave me Lake Michigan.

...

In the 1940s and '50s, Gary was booming. With the Gary Works operating at its peak with as many as twenty thousand employees, it became the region's center of commerce and industry. It was known variously as the "Steel City," "America's Magic Industrial City," or "City of the Century." The industrial and urban upheavals of the late 20th century, however, ruined all that and sent Gary into a steep decline. "The seeds for the decline were contained in decades of rigid segregation and suppression of the African-Americans in housing and in schools and in the dispersal of white residents to new suburbs after World War II" (Glass, *Indianapolis Star*). Many of its problems were also self-inflicted—"bloated payrolls, warlike labor relations, obsolete equipment . . ." (Young, *Chicago Tribune*). It became very difficult, therefore, to compete with the forces of globalization.

According to the author of *Lost Gary:* "Its once steely reputation has been lost to time, neglect, and politics, forever tarnished as the rusted face of urban decay. Only one other American city, Detroit, has hit such rock bottom" (Davich, 14). Gary and Detroit are acute cases of conditions in the industrial Midwest. Detroit is struggling to recover. But according to *Lost Gary*, the city seems to be a lost city of abandoned dreams and abandoned neighborhoods. A December 2019 publication even described it as "The Most Miserable City in America."

U.S. Steel still operates the Gary Works, the corporation's largest facility, but its employment levels have fallen drastically—from twenty thousand in the 1970s to five thousand in 2015. The Gary Works remains, however, one of northwest Indiana's largest employers. *The Times of Northwest Indiana* reported on March 15, 2021, that "the steel market has been rebounding after automakers resumed production." The company restarted blast furnace #4 and began recalling laid-off workers. Nevertheless, the Gary Works is not what it was in the boom years.

Once "the premiere healthcare facility in Gary," Mercy Hospital closed in 1995. Its fortunes depended on the rise and fall of steel. As steel declined and the mill's employees and city population did as well, the hospital began contracting. By 1993, it was in "financial dire straits" and then by 1995, "it was drowning in debt" (*Sometimesinteresting.com*). It had struggled for years, but the effects of a declining, depressed city were too much. The Gary Police Department now occupies the newer part of Mercy built in the parking lot across from my grandparents' home. The old part has been abandoned and is "beyond repair"—like so much of Gary.

And my grandparents' house and neighborhood? The entire block of Polk Street between 5th and 6th Avenues is now a parking lot. 536 Polk Street is nothing but a site of memory and history—and parking.

• • •

Gary now is largely an African American city with less than half the population of its peak years. I'm uneasy leaving my description of it as a kind of "ruin"—uneasy that *Lost Gary* is simply a white man's reading of the city. The author closes his book: "Returning to Gary this past year with a fresh outlook and renewed perspective, I discovered a new understanding and a new appreciation for the city." (Mainly for what it once was.) "Yes, it's in shambles in many ways. Yes, its challenges outweigh its resources. Yes, it can be sad to return there again and again." But then he urges us to return "with a similar fresh outlook . . . Look to the past" (Davich, 122). The present for him is indeed a ruin. In expressing uneasiness, however, I do not want to indulge simply in white guilt, reluctant to see the city for what it is.

In 2019, Karen Freeman-Wilson, an African American and Gary's mayor, said that Gary is at once seriously challenged and also engaged in active redevelopment. "Since 2012, we have been operating with millions less in property tax dollars, imposed property tax caps, a skyrocketing vacancy rate, unemployment rate and with very few investments. Today, we have realized new investments through federal, state and county dollars, grants and through partnerships . . . We have also ushered in a new era of nonprofit investment through our participation in national initiatives that have led to tangible positive outcomes and opportunities for our residents." Near the end of the "miserable" piece, the writer acknowledges something positive: "Though the town is slowly coming back from its collapse, it looks like it will need a lot more time before it can shake off its ghost town reputation" (*allthatisinteresting.com*).

Whatever the "correct" version of the city might be, Gary no longer resembles the place where my grandparents lived and I remember. It is that Gary, my grandparents' city, their Polk Street house and property at Ogden Dunes, the South Shore Railroad, Chicago and baseball—every aspect of my history there that set my lifelong fascination with Lake Michigan. And that is both a blessing and a curse. I delight in these memories. I love the lake. I go there as often as I can. At the same time, I cannot escape. Its absence, my sense of loss, burdens me and keeps me from investing fully elsewhere.

• 3 •

Water 1

"I cannot sit beside a stream without falling into a profound reverie."
Gaston Bachelard

Who has not sensed the magic, the mesmerizing appeal of water, even if it's only a creek or branch flowing down a mountainside; a small pond reflecting a blue sky, clouds moving across, casting shadows on the surface; an inland lake—diving off a dock, pushing away in a rowboat or canoe, pulling the starter cord on an outboard, casting a line far out; the torrent of water crashing down a mountainside at the spring thaw; the vastness of the Great Lakes, inland seas, and the oceans; or just rain—spatter, drizzle, downpour; the quiet trickle in a small fountain or the explosion of water in a large one? The sights, scents, sounds, sensations of water—it is magic indeed.

    I think of Roxanne and Rosalind, my golden retrievers, slurping water from the small branch flowing from a spring further up the mountain—I gaze and listen to the water, splashing over rocks and flowing through the watercress, the sunlight striking the surface until my dogs pull me away; of family picnics on wide, flat rocks along the Olentangy River, or further away on a grassy slope beside the wider and deeper Scioto River; the creek at my grandfather's farm, down a steep hillside, where we wade, swim, or simply sit or walk by the water; hiking along the Delaware Run past Blue Limestone Lake and the B&O Railroad tracks, on out of town, passing behind Jane Case Hospital, staying always along the creek; a two-day float on the Pine River from the interior of northern

Michigan to Manistee, where the river opens into Lake Michigan; a week of camping and canoeing in Killarney Provincial Park—portaging from one small lake to another. Alone and always near, on, or in water. Then Lake Michigan.

These—and so many others— are modest moments at insignificant places, but water makes them memorable. Water lures me time and again. Water, always water, and the magic Melville describes.

I am hardly an Ishmael: "Some years ago—having little or no money in my purse, and nothing particular to interest me on shore, I thought I would sail about a little and see the watery part of the world. It is a way I have of driving off the spleen, and regulating the circulation" (*Moby Dick*, 795). My adventures have not been nearly so dramatic and long, but some have been therapeutic—a watery experience I share with Ishmael. During especially trying times in Michigan, I would sit by the Red Cedar River to calm myself—to forget momentarily. Surely Lake Michigan calmed me and my four daughters on what I remember as the most beautiful day in the world.

Nor am I a Melville recording his voyages as he did first in *Typee*: "Six months at sea! Yes, reader, as I live, six months out of sight of land; cruising after the sperm-whale beneath the scorching sun of the Line, and tossed on the billows of the wide-rolling Pacific—the sky above, the sea around, and nothing else!" (11). The oceans—water—compelled him to go.

Neither an Ishmael nor a Melville am I. However, I remain one of those impelled "waterward," transfixed by the magic of water. We seek the calm, the peace, the happiness of being near water. Wallace Nichols has given the impulse a name: "Blue Mind, a mildly meditative state characterized by calm, peacefulness, unity, and a sense of general happiness and satisfaction with life in the moment" (6). He describes a great deal of scientific research that substantiates this reaction.

When I think about the whole story of the Pequod and Ishmael, however, "I only am escaped alone to tell thee" (1408), I realize that water also possesses a dark or black magic. Water both consoles and intimidates, creates and destroys, purifies and poisons.

• 4 •

Rediscovering Lake Michigan

"I wish you water."
Wallace Nichols, *Blue Mind*

As an older teenager and young adult, I visited the lakes from time to time: Lake Erie with my friend David Smith's family; Lake Huron when my uncle lived in Rogers City, Michigan; an inland lake in lower Wisconsin. I loved being on the beach, swimming in the chilly water, watching waves break into whitecaps far out, hearing and seeing waves lap or crash onto the beach, feeling the warm sun on my face and shoulders, inhaling the clean freshwater scent, and observing the different surface colors as the sun's angle changed through the day or clouds cast shadows on the water. It was all ideal, but only that. I did not know how possessed I was—or would be—by Lake Michigan. Those feelings lay deeply dormant—until I moved to East Lansing in 1966 with JoAnn, my first wife, and our four daughters.

That move returned me to the lake I'd been away from for years. We could drive there in less than two hours—and except for the first two years, we'd go several times each summer to P. J. Hoffmaster State Park near Muskegon—a park of beautiful beaches, high sand dunes, hiking trails, and camping sites. We didn't camp, but at least once we stayed overnight at a Holiday Inn—all six of us squeezed into one large room. We ordered pizza and ate in the room, not knowing much about area restaurants and not having much money for dining out. Normally, we'd make day trips, taking beach chairs, towels, and blankets, and spending long hours swimming, sunning, and sleeping. From the observation deck at the top, we could see far out into the lake. As far south in Michigan as Hoffmaster is, the water temperature rarely reached seventy degrees, and not until August. But active daughters and their young parents—I was thirty-one when we moved—enjoyed the lake and depended on the sun for warmth.

...

During our first summer in Michigan, I read almost every day about wretched conditions on the beaches. An alewife, or river herring, population had exploded in the 1960s. In 1962, the alewife constituted 17 percent of the fishery; by the mid-'60s, it was 90 percent. They dominated the food chain from bottom to top by consuming plankton and preying on young trout. The native fishery then collapsed as it had once before under a previous attack. By the mid-1960s, the lake no longer could support so many, and that caused a massive die-off. Billions of dead alewives littered Lake Michigan beaches. In 1967, alewife carcasses were piled up along three hundred miles of Lake Michigan shoreline. "The joke on the lakefront then," according to one local, was, "'there's a pile of them. It's six inches deep, six feet wide, and three hundred miles long" (Lavey, June 6, 2016). Only it wasn't so much of a joke. The carcasses and stench made the beaches virtually unusable. As much as the lake might have called, we didn't go for two summers. The entire tourist industry suffered. It was an environmental disaster.

Originally, the alewives were an East Coast fish that spawned in fresh water. It isn't altogether clear how they entered Lake Ontario and then colonized the upper Great Lakes. Through the Erie Canal? The Welland? Stocked by mistake? But some presumably beneficial human action exposed the lakes to their invasion.

Within a few years, state biologists discovered a solution. They stocked the lake waters with thousands of coho salmon. The salmon preyed on alewives. Within a year, no dead ones blighted the beaches. The population was declining. The coho flourished. They made great game fish and caused a salmon craze, as fishermen crowded to the lake to fish for this exotic new species. The Lake Michigan fishery was transformed from commercial to sport fishing. The western Michigan economy benefited enormously. In 1967, "Lake Michigan was bursting with nearly two million planted coho" (Egan, 95). The same year, Michigan biologists introduced some eight hundred thousand chinook salmon into Lakes Michigan and Superior. It is a larger and easier to raise fish. It became "the linchpin of Lake Michigan sport fishing . . . It's big, it's aggressive, and it's good eating" (Lavey, *Lansing State Journal*).

Before the alewives and my time in Michigan, there had been an equally disastrous invasion of non-native, predatory "fish." Until the opening of the Welland Canal in 1835 between Lakes Erie and Ontario, the upper Great Lakes were isolated and protected. The canal benefitted travel and commerce. But it opened the region to a rapid population growth. In just fifty years, Chicago grew from about thirty thousand residents to 1.7 million. The expansion of agriculture and lumbering stripped the land of forests, changed erosion and runoff patterns, and allowed a greater flow of nutrients and sediments into the lakes. This was the pollution that existed in the 1930s and '40s. Even if we'd known in those early years when we were so captivated by the Ogden Dunes beach, we doubtless would have behaved in the same way: go to the beach and swim.

The canal also opened the lakes to sea lampreys, first found in Lake Ontario in 1835, but not in destructive numbers. A later expansion of the Welland allowed lampreys to move past the Niagara escarpment and invade the upper lakes. Over time, these eel-like bloodsuckers—"one of nature's most devastating and durable predators" (Egan, 46)—virtually eliminated the lake trout and whitefish that had dominated commercial fishing for decades. In just ten years, from the 1940s through the '50s, the lake trout harvest collapsed from a take of 6.5 million pounds to zero. The whitefish catch also declined sharply.

THE LAKE EFFECT

To solve that problem, scientists developed a poison that killed sea lampreys but did not harm the native fishery—except for lake sturgeon, sacred to a group of Ottawas. And over the years, the toxic chemical did kill a fair number of young sturgeon. I'm not sure the Ottawas' problem was ever resolved. The poison reduced the lampreys to a manageable 10 percent of what they'd been. It was an elaborate process that focused on lamprey spawning grounds in rivers and streams that flowed into Lake Michigan. The native fishery recovered, but then came the alewives.

• • •

I knew the beaches were unusable in the mid-1960s. The news reports and warnings made that clear. But I knew little else about how threatened the lakes really were and would become. I was simply captivated by the wonder and beauty of this Great Lake. After those first two years, we went as often as we could on outings that did not differ, I assume, from the way many families spent days at the beach and on the Great Lakes. All quite ordinary. It's what you do. It's fun and strangely irresistible.

• • •

Even our family camping fiasco on Lake Superior was what you do. We'd heard about the charming village of Grand Marais in the Upper Peninsula and the beautiful bay there. Without much thought about camping gear, weather, or any other practical matter, we decided to go. We borrowed old sleeping bags, blankets, tents, and camping equipment from my stepfather—it was all old, very old. We were driving a cheap Ford van that didn't even have interior door and side panels covering the metal. It was so light that moderate winds rocked and sometimes almost pushed it off the road. Lake Superior was a good twelve hours away from my mother's home. We camped one night along the route. By then, a severe poison ivy rash had erupted on my legs and was driving me crazy. We arrived in Grand Marais on a sunny, mild afternoon—very promising. We set up camp. JoAnn and I would sleep in the tent. The girls would sleep packed in the van—two on seats, one on the floor between the seats, and dear Becky on the floor inside the rear doors and behind a seat. I shudder to think about that confinement. We managed one night reasonably well.

The next day a strong (and unexpected by us) cold front blew through. We'd prepared for summer, but not for a Lake Superior late summer. We headed to the general store to buy jackets and gloves—much to the amusement, I expect, of the locals. With the temperature dropping fast into the high thirties, however, sweaters, mittens, and jackets did not help. We were chilled through. "This is awful," we agreed. "We're miserable." So, we broke camp, left Grand Marais, and drove all night back to my mother's and stepfather's house in Ohio—back to summer as we thought it should be.

• • •

Of all the family experiences at Lake Michigan, I remember one exceptional day. I think of it as the most beautiful day in the world. I don't remember the details—a loss I regret, but the meaning of the day impressed me deeply. Unfortunately, none of my daughters recall it at all. When I ask and tell them why, they look at me blankly. Maybe they don't remember because it was a rare day—unique for them, as well as for me. The five of us—myself, Lindy, Becky, Ginny, and Janey—drove to Lake Michigan for a day outing. JoAnn and I were no longer together. For the two hours each way and for several at Hoffmaster, everyone behaved in unimaginably pleasant ways. No bickering. No attacking one another. No pushing or shoving. No tears or anger. Lindy did not harass her youngest sister or call her "shortz," "wart," or "bubble butt." Ginny felt calm—no tears or screaming. Becky remained her usual quiet, observant self—as did Janey, the youngest. I don't remember what exactly we did at the beach or where or what we ate. I just think of it as an exquisite day. My daughters, aware or not, seemed determined to make it as pleasant for "Daddy" as possible, given all the torment of separation and divorce. It *was* the most beautiful day in the world. Perhaps it was simply our Blue Minds taking over.

The most beautiful day in the world

It took years for me to understand Lake Michigan's captivating presence and emotional force or all the ways the lakes have been compromised—to understand what I'm writing about, insofar as I do. My professional life was progressing nicely. My family life had broken apart. My attachment to Lake Michigan continued. My second and late wife, Barbara, shared my fascination with the lake. Its power and presence grew stronger and stronger.

• 5 •

Lake Michigan Rising

"A New Normal ... uncharted territory"
Gronewold and Rood

Every summer for twenty years, Barbara and I rented a house on Lake Michigan—an A-frame near Whitehall one year; a cottage high on a dune near Pentwater another summer; an old beach house on the isthmus between Lake Michigan and White Lake; a friend's summer house outside Suttons Bay and across the road from Grand Traverse Bay; an Old Mission place overlooking the East Bay; and others lost to time.

The A-frame rested on a high bluff overlooking the lake. Except for the seventy-five steps down to the beach and the 175 (it seemed) back up, the house was beautifully located and not far from a cottage owned by my friend Lee Winder, the Michigan State University provost I worked with.

The old beach house was razed after we'd rented it. As much as we would have liked to return another summer, we obviously couldn't. One evening that summer, the Winders came to dinner. Afterwards, Lee and I were sitting near the edge of White Lake. We watched a sailboat come through the channel from the big lake to drop anchor for the night. The couple on board then stripped and in classic skinny-dip form, plunged into the lake. Lee and I smiled. "Well, how about that!" Fortunately (for them or us?) they'd anchored a prudent distance offshore. We did not have binoculars.

We rented the Suttons Bay house, on the Leelanau Peninsula, from a friend and colleague of Barbara's. That house, like the others, assuaged my longing but hardly satisfied it. That summer, I was revising my book manuscript about Loren Eiseley for the University of Illinois Press. It was not going well. I became so discouraged and frustrated at one point, I threw the entire manuscript across the room. Barbara then said, "This is driving you crazy—and unnerving me, so let me edit it." She did and helped make it work. That made our Suttons Bay and lake time much more pleasant.

• • •

Every summer we also fantasized about owning a place on the lake. We asked a northern Michigan friend once, "How do you acquire Lake Michigan property?" "Just hope your grandparents bought it," he said with a smile. Cost was obviously the issue. Nevertheless, every summer we looked at nearby cottages and houses for sale—dreaming we might find a way. One summer, we came close. It was a wonderful lake house with five bedrooms, several baths, a wide screened-in sleeping porch on the second floor, a wide veranda off the main floor, a good kitchen, two new furnaces, the house resting on a new masonry foundation, and best of all, one hundred feet of lakefront and a reasonable price—$89,000. What held us back? Money, to be sure, but more than that: Lake Michigan was rising as the lakes do rhythmically over time. High water and waves wash out beaches, erode dunes, and undermine cottages. Down the beach to the left, two or three structures had tipped or fallen into the lake. This "perfect" house had been moved back once from the edge of the dune—which explained the new foundation and furnaces. Its beach had been washed away. The water was still rising. We could not know how much more of the dune would be lost, how close to the edge the house would be. Still, we were tempted enough to see it a second time and keep in touch with the realtor after we'd returned to East Lansing.

Several days later a flyer listing the house arrived from the realtor with a large "SELL" scrawled across it and a price of $69,000 scrawled across the list price of $89,000. How could we not buy that? That's $240,000 in 2022 dollars—a ridiculously low price for a house on Lake Michigan. Well, we didn't—money and high water. The house did not fall into the lake. The water receded within a few years. The beaches reappeared. The house repossessed one hundred feet of wide, sandy beach directly on the lake. I tell this story of loss over and over with a smile of regret and resignation—and self-irony—to anyone who will listen. Just one more lost opportunity.

...

I am describing Lake Michigan in the early 1980s. But the rhythm of rising and falling lake levels continues. It is, after all, a natural phenomenon. The Great Lakes have risen and fallen since they were formed after the Ice Age. In the summer of 2019, Lake Michigan stood close to a record high. It had risen seven feet from an extreme low in 2013 to this high level in just six years. Over the last twenty, the lake had risen and fallen and risen again to four feet above its average. A year later it rose even further. Winter snows and spring and summer rain have increased noticeably. By the fall of 2019, the Great Lakes had experienced a fifth straight wettest year on record. Lake Michigan reached still another record high in 2020. For all I know the house we didn't buy might have been damaged or lost in these recent high-water years.

One homeowner reported that his beach is gone; his wooden stairway "lies in a twisted, crumpled heap . . . at the bottom of a steep, 40- to 50-foot cliff." He's losing large chunks of land "worth about $13,000 a linear foot." It's an economic, as well as an aesthetic loss. He also reported that some people lost their homes altogether. "What was really a retirement paradise for a lot of people has become a nightmare, unfortunately" (Matheny, *Detroit Free Press*).

Such rapid changes in lake levels represents a new normal, according to hydrology and climate scientists:

> Our view is based on interactions between global climate variability and the components of the regional hydrological cycle. Increasing precipitation, the threat of recurring periods of high evaporation, and a combination of both routine and unusual climate events—such as extreme cold air outbursts—are putting the region in uncharted territory . . . More winter precipitation is falling, often as snow. The snow is melting earlier in response to rising temperatures and shorter winters. The resulting runoff is then amplified in years like 2019 with large springtime rains (Gronewald and Rood).

Moreover, it seems that temperatures in the Great Lakes region are rising faster than elsewhere in North America. Climate change seems to be influencing the lakes, but to what extent no one really knows. We are making the history that will inform others in the future about the effects of climate change.

. . .

In 2019, my wife, Beth, and I dealt with high water in a small way when we rented kayaks for an outing on Spring Lake—the small lake near Grand Haven that opens into Lake Michigan. We didn't understand why we had to park in a church lot, a five-to-ten-minute walk from the kayak rental office, until we saw the foot of water covering its parking lot. We walked to the office over temporary, wooden ramps. Once on Spring Lake, we paddled by docks fallen into the water, submerged footpaths, and flooded yards. These effects inconvenience and cost individual homeowners, to be sure. Some pay up to $200,000, sometimes even more, to protect their properties from erosion, or repair damage already done, by installing seawalls, riprap, or groins.

While "armoring" shorelines might temporarily hold back the lakes, it can also redirect waves and water and thereby accelerate erosion. Even the strongest seawalls will eventually give way. There's a certain futility in armoring. "It pains me," said Guy Meadows, director of the Marine Engineering Laboratory at Michigan Technological University. "People build a revetment, it does not hold up, and they will build a bigger revetment, and an even bigger revetment, until the cost of the revetment exceeds the value of the property." Jerrod Sanders, assistant director of the Michigan Department of Environment, Great Lakes, and Energy, made the long term futility quite clear: "You're building a structure in one of the most inhospitable places on the planet" (*Bridge Michigan*).

House sliding into Lake Michigan *(Photo by Cory Morse, MLive Media Group)*

Some owners even move houses back from the edge of a dune at considerable cost—like the house I looked at in the 1980s. We try to manage nature over and over and at best succeed only for the moment and at great expense.

THE LAKE EFFECT

The costs to cities and towns are much greater. I'm writing now about 2019. The next year turned out to be the same, if not worse. In Leland, people were trying to save Fishtown, a historic fishing village on the Leelanau Peninsula. Its quaint shanties were being undermined by high water. The oldest one, built in 1903, had been flooded and was unusable. The floors in the other two could rot from repeated flooding. Fishtown supports Leland's tourist economy. Had high water and then winter ice further damaged the shanties, the town would have suffered. They survived, however. In the summer of 2021, tourists flooded the town, not high water.

Manistee had to raise docks at its marinas and deal with shoreline erosion along the channel between the big lake and Manistee Lake. The boat launches in town were still usable, but the docks were submerged. The city closed a stairway to the beach because of erosion. Winter could bring even more damage from storms driving water and ice further on shore.

In Ludington, just south of Manistee, city workers had to pump lake water out of flooded storm sewers over and over. The overflow spilled onto streets and sidewalks. It was, as one newspaper reported, a "thankless, endless task" that probably would not prevent serious infrastructure damage. That was a cost, as well as an inconvenience, for an entire city.

A short drive south of Ludington, rising water in Pentwater made an inland bridge inaccessible. So, the town bought a sixteen-passenger ferry, the Lake Sturgeon, and offered free rides across Pentwater Lake from one side of town to the other. This saved people a long detour around the lake. It was also a real cost to a small village of 850 people. There were other area inconveniences and costs, as well. Longbridge Road was closed for months because the Oceana County Road Commission feared high water in the Pentwater River was weakening the road's foundation. Other roads, as well, were closed to prevent further damage to the roadways and danger to motorists.

At Ogden Dunes along the south rim of Lake Michigan, beach erosion had accelerated. People feared their houses might fall into the lake or never sell because of possible structural damage and disappearing beaches. The town estimated that by 2018 it had lost 80 percent of the beach it had in 2010. "The beach is decimated," wrote Morgan Greene, a reporter for the *Chicago Tribune*. "It is so unnerving," Steve Coombs, an Ogden Dunes resident, said. Coombs worried about losing his house (Smith, *The New York Times*).

"It's heart-wrenching. You don't ever want to see someone's house go into the lake," said Richard Norton, a professor of urban and regional planning. It will probably cost the town millions of dollars to fix the problems. And that assumes the lake will recede in a few years. The situation is especially severe at Ogden Dunes because of all the industrial development along the shore that has interrupted the natural flow of lake and sand. Another resident said, "It really comes down to the survival of our town," (Greene, *Chicago Tribune*).

High water was causing problems in virtually every town and city along the Lake Michigan shoreline. I've cited just a few 2019 examples. Thought of on that scale, the lake's level caused a monumental problem. When people think about winter and the potential for a massive ice buildup along the lakeshore, the problem is even more imposing. In average years, I've seen "ice mountains" along the shore that are five, ten, fifteen feet high. Wind and waves constantly throw water on the beach and then on the ice, and gradually over the cold months the ice piles up and up. I can imagine even greater erosion and damage to roads, seawalls, docks, beaches, and houses, by ice from the high lake level.

The rising and falling rhythm continues as it has for centuries. In February 2022, e.g., Lake Michigan had fallen two feet below its 2020 record high. It was an unusually dry January. By April, the lake was just six inches above its average. Through the year, however, it will rise, but how much isn't clear. On April 1, the Army Corps projected a four-inch rise over the month. The rise and fall of water levels will depend on weather conditions. Warming and cooling, rain, snow, evaporation, new construction, greater runoff, and climate change will influence lake levels, but even those factors do not account entirely for changes in water level. We are living in the "new normal." "Things have changed dramatically due to the climate. And it's hard to know what the future is going to bring"—other than rising and falling water and uncertainty (Fox 17). "Predicting outcomes with any certainty is nearly impossible. I know that isn't satisfying, but that is how things work" (Mann, *Lakeland Boating*).

...

Whether it is summer water and wave damage or the effects of winter ice buildup, the lake does lose some of its easy romantic appeal. I say that, but then remember how impressive and beautiful the power of water and ice can be. And I recall times I went to the lake in midwinter—especially one cold February day at Glen Haven; another, watching and listening to the ice along the lakeshore; and then a cold February day sitting on a low dune near Saugatuck. We were, in each instance, simply learning more and more about the lake and lakeshore towns—what it's like in winter.

Located on the Leelanau Peninsula, Glen Haven is a tiny, now uninhabited, village in the Sleeping Bear National Lakeshore. Once an active port serving the timber industry as well as general shipping, Glen Haven lost its economy and eventually its population. The National Park Service bought the village in the 1970s and restored the main buildings. From Memorial Day to Labor Day, the Cannery Boathouse operates as a small boat museum; the old General Store serves tourists; and the Blacksmith Shop offers demonstrations. The Sleeping Bear Inn opened in 1857 and closed in 1973. It remains, however, a handsome two-story building that captures my imagination—what might it have been like staying there at its height? One day soon, however, I might in fact be able to stay there. The inn has been leased for restoration as a B&B.

Glen Haven is located on a large cove on Lake Michigan and looks toward the Manitou Islands. They lie twelve miles offshore from Leland, Michigan, and are part of the National Lakeshore. The Manitou Island ferry from Leland serves them. The two islands have interesting and rich histories beginning with Native American fishing, followed much later by lumbering in the 19th century; then active farming; and later as hunting and fishing resorts. They're now open to hiking and camping and for visits to historic and cultural sites: the lighthouse on South Manitou; the U.S. Life Saving Service National Historic Landmark on North Manitou; Cottage Row in the Village on North Manitou, once an active residential area; old farmsteads on South Manitou; a 1927 sawmill similar to the one used for 19th-century lumbering; an old orchard; and even a cemetery. No one lives on the Manitous now. There is a ranger station on South Manitou with restrooms. As of spring 2020, the only potable water on the islands was at the ranger station.

In winter, Glen Haven is a virtual ghost town. No vehicles, no people were there on the frigid February day I drove to it. The day was brilliantly clear. I could easily see the Manitous. The cove wasn't frozen over completely, but the ice extended quite far out. It was building up along the beach. There was deep snow everywhere. I looked in the windows of the inn and tried to imagine enjoying a hot drink, seated in the comfortable furniture of the public rooms, warmed by a wood fire of local lumber. It was an enchanting, memorable day. In any season, Glen Haven is a beautiful place. No wonder people settled there. No surprise it draws tourists all summer long.

• • •

It was another clear, cold, February day, in a different year. The temperature had been rising slowly after days of intense cold from an arctic air mass. The ice along the shore had built up considerably with peaks and valleys like miniature mountain ranges extending thirty to forty yards beyond the beach into the lake. The day was calm and quiet. The movement of the water and air was barely discernible. At first, I didn't notice, but as I stood silently looking out over the ice to the lake, I heard a faint creaking, scraping sound. A sheet of ice no thicker than window glass had formed on the flat water beyond the ice. The almost imperceptible movement of the water was pushing the thin sheets against the big ice. The pressure broke the thin ice into pieces that resembled broken window glass, and then stacked it in layers as one might stack pieces of glass against a wall or the side of a building. I'd never seen or heard anything like the straining and cracking and breaking of a thin sheet of ice.

After a light thaw and then another cold snap the lake started freezing again. I went back. Most of the mounds and ridges had broken up during the brief thaw. They extended only five to ten yards from the beach, but the flatter ice reached out much farther. The pieces of snow and ice from the breakup had frozen together to form a wide and rough expanse of snow and snow-encrusted ice difficult to walk on. This newly formed ice field wasn't wide where I started, but in a small bay around a point, ice appeared to fill the bay. I walked along the edge, close to shore, fearing that farther out the ice might not be strong enough to hold me. I didn't go far. It was very cold, and walking was slow and awkward. The wind blew harder than a few days before. Waves of two to three feet rolled slowly and quietly against the edge of the ice, causing the floating fragments to rise and fall. The cold soon drove me back to the warmth of the car.

• • •

We sat on a low dune along the lakeshore and watched the sun set. This was in the mid-1990s. Huddled in our down coats, shielding ourselves from twenty-five degrees and a brisk wind, Barbara (my late wife) said, "If we should come here to live someday, this is what it would be like along the lake—at least in winter." The sun settled into the lake behind light clouds. The horizon line was sharp, the color striking. A rich red suffused the western sky. We'd been there an hour, and so well-chilled, we left quickly after the sunset. During that hour, we saw few others on the beach. A single runner appeared far to our right—a dark figure way up the beach coming in our direction. He approached, turned into the break in the dune next to us, and ran on up the path without a nod or notice. Two men emerged from the path while we sat there—one probably in his fifties, wearing only a sport coat, V-neck sweater,

and an open-collared shirt. The younger man was wearing a light windbreaker. They walked to the water's edge, stood talking for maybe ten minutes, then left by the same path. How could they stand even ten minutes? Then almost at sundown, a bearded man, his long gray hair pulled back, and his dog passed, heading south along the shore. He didn't notice us, either. I didn't feel the rush of longing and sadness I've felt sometimes at the lake, just the satisfaction of being there in spite of the discomfort.

Even in this cold, we indulged our fantasy about a house—this time as a place to live. We imagined three possibilities: lakefront in a beautiful residential area south of Saugatuck—doubtless beyond our means; a handsome older community across the road, where it runs along a high bluff and gives a splendid view of Lake Michigan—ideal, but with houses then at $350,000, probably beyond us; or in a small town like Saugatuck with easy access to the lake. We'd look, again, the following summer—knowing it would be entertainment, but probably not a serious search, although we couldn't know for sure.

. . .

How easily I am carried away by the haunting beauty of the lake in winter and these memorable moments, but enough. I find myself on the verge of a usual mistake—failing to balance the romantic with the real. So, I return to the shelf ice and its forbidding power—especially in years of high water. Wind and water pushing ice on shore could cause further erosion and damage to docks, sea walls, or riprap, boathouses, and marinas.

Shelf ice also poses a danger to anyone who risks walking on it. One could easily fall through an ice shaft into unbearably cold water. There's no way to climb back up a long, slippery shaft. Some are three feet in diameter and over fifteen feet deep. Sudden immersion makes breathing very difficult. Muscles contract from the shock of the cold water. Gasping for breath could draw in water instead of air. Death by drowning might well occur. "If your winter plans," an official advises, "include a visit to the frozen shores of the Great Lakes, enjoy the spectacular scenes from a safe distance. Stay on the shore, and away from any slippery surfaces near the water. And never, ever walk on the shelf ice. It's beautiful, but potentially deadly (Hillman-Rapley). There is nothing romantic or beautiful about that version of shelf ice.

• 6 •

Water 2

WORDS AND IMAGES

"And I wanted the words to put it all together—every place, every moment, and all they signified . . . It had become overwhelming. The water alone was defeating me. How do you describe water?"
Jerry Dennis

Jerry Dennis has written with great skill, knowledge, and effect about the Great Lakes in several books. I share his sense of the difficulty of describing water. Lake Michigan is even more forbidding. Its many avatars pose a problem for me—perhaps for anyone trying to write about the lake. I've been haunted by its beauty and its mystery most of my life—the magic Melville speaks of. When I write about that, I'm immersed in a discourse of sentiment and romance—a limited, but necessary, aesthetic language. We do, we must, find ways to enjoy and express life's beauty and pleasure. How could we stand it otherwise? But serious writers, I've been told, "can no longer say it that way"—that is, write only about beauty and enchantment in a conventional discourse. There is, after all, Captain Ahab and the white whale and the long history of human incursion and environmental degradation of the lake, not to speak of life's bleak and painful realities. We must now write with realism and irony and subvert simplistic notions of beauty, or find an altogether different vocabulary for the Great Lakes and water.

Dennis continues: "What words can evoke those spangles of sunlight, those shifting wave shadows, those pellucid blue depths? I lacked the vocabulary. I wanted to take hold of the immediate world, see it independent of the names we give it, then give it name. But I couldn't grasp it" (*The Living Great Lakes,* 9). He isn't simply looking for the right words—the bon mots. I hear, instead, a desire for an altogether new way of writing about the lakes and water because the conventional discourse fails to grasp the full reality of Lake Michigan or of the Great Lakes. I also hear a desire to capture it all—to grasp the lake in some final way. I share that impulse from time to time. But I'm aware, as I expect Jerry Dennis is, that we cannot grasp it all in any sense.

It is the social discourse—the semantics and grammar of the language we are raised within and then live—that fails us even in describing what we can. It guides us to see and speak in certain, limited ways—often in a sentimental way about the lake and nature. We write *only* about Melville's "magic." Or the available discourse simply limits our capacity to perceive fully or differently. Conventional discourse, for example, guides us to see and say, "the sun is setting." From a fixed, unmoving place we see the sun go down. It's like we still live in a Ptolemaic world.

Only once did I escape that perception and terminology. I'd rented a cottage, high on a dune, facing Lake Michigan. For days the unusually hot weather and biting flies made the first week unpleasant. Nevertheless, I was at the lake. Then one evening I stepped outside myself and that way of perception. I was standing on the lakeshore—as I had so many times—just one more beautiful night. The sun was slowly setting, streaking the sky in brilliant red, orange, purple, gray. And then it wasn't setting. I felt deep within me that I, the beach, and the lake were turning away from the sun—rolling away into the dark of night. It was an Earth-turn, not a sunset. I was sober and rational, and then I wasn't—caught up in a mystical moment beyond reason—except that it wasn't. That's what in fact happens: a lake, a state, a continent turns away, rolls away, from the sun. But I felt it viscerally. I could almost hear it. I was indeed

Sunset on Lake Michigan

rolling away—away from my ordinary self back there on the beach and beyond conventional perception and terminology—turning toward darkness, mystery, another world.

A small example, but it makes my point about the limits of our discourse and the way it guides perception. So how *do* I write it differently? How do I capture this complex, layered, even contradictory mosaic? I am writing, in a sense, alternatively, ironically, discontinuously—all to achieve that oppositional mode Glück identifies.

Even if we believe we've found the words, sentences, style, and rhythms to capture the lake in all its different features, functions, and forces, Lake Michigan and the Great Lakes constantly exceed our grasp. When my German friends Ludwig and Brigitta first saw the lake, they said, "But you can't see across it." Our words can't see across it, either.

Jerry Dennis writes about this, as well: "I was reaching for something else entirely. I wanted to hold what I saw, felt, heard, tasted, and scented, and to possess it always—not like a tourist snapping photos, but literally, taking possession of its physical fact and keeping it with me always—yet I couldn't get my arms around it" (*The Living Great Lakes*, 10). He seems to be saying that he couldn't quite get his words around it. But he has come as close as anyone.

So, we reach for it all and grasp what we can. Dennis certainly captures a great deal through his presence along, on, and in the lake and through his artfulness as a writer. My experience differs significantly from his. Mine begins at age two, as you've read. Over the decades I've had many direct, immediate experiences with the lake, but it has been present in my life often through its absence. So, my writing speaks of return and departure and of recovery and loss.

• • •

Gaston Bachelard speaks to the relationship of words and water in his conclusion to "Water's Voice." "*Liquidity* is, in my opinion, the very desire of language. Language needs to flow." He is writing primarily about poetry and the correspondence between language and the material world. I read (or extend) him to suggest that those who write about water—Lake Michigan in my case—should achieve the liquidity of water. "Water is the mistress of liquid language, of smooth flowing language, of continued and continuing language, of language that softens rhythm" (187). I don't pretend to write poetry in these pages, but his notion that "language must be filled with water" suggests that words and water somehow flow together in a style or discourse unknown to me (192). I'm not sure how literal the intertwining is for Bachelard—the "*correspondence* between words and reality"— but as metaphor, it sets an expectation (189). Who wouldn't write not just fluently but fluidly, if we only could?

A liquid, flowing prose, however, could be an elegant, enchanting version of a conventional romantic or sentimental discourse. Fluidity might hold for Bachelard's notion that "water is also a model of calm and silence" (192). The "magic" of Melville, perhaps. Or the peace and calm of the Blue Mind. But how then should we write about violent water that disrupts and destroys? Water that in Bachelard's terms can also be our adversary—our opponent in a combat. He quotes George Lafourcade: "The sea is an enemy who seeks to vanquish and whom we must vanquish" (167). Do we write still fluidly in a conventional discourse, or as I suggest ironically or discontinuously—in a way that interrupts a "liquid" description of calmness? Do we find a way of intertwining the two opposites—calm and silence with violence? Or as I am attempting, do we place these separate moments in the lake's mosaic so that they flow together in the wholeness of the lake, yet at the same time remain distinct as pieces in a mosaic?

...

I've been thinking about the challenges of representing the many faces of the lake and water in words—in language or discourse. It's my version of the general problem of representation. The time-bound character of language—its linearity—affects its capacity to represent the lake. After writing or reading over time—page to page, chapter to chapter, detail after detail—we might in the end develop a sense of the complex whole that is Lake Michigan or the Great Lakes. And it might be finely textured. But it will have been an extended process.

By contrast, the simultaneity of representation in Alex Rockman's "The Great Lakes Cycle" paintings gives us the lakes in beautiful, complex, visual imagery. In 2013 the Grand Rapids Art Museum invited Rockman to begin research for the "Cycle." The exhibition of the resulting art opened at the museum in 2018. The core of "The Great Lakes Cycle" consists of a suite of five six-by-twelve-foot panoramic paintings depicting the past and present of the Great Lakes, their beauty and majesty, their many features and functions, human interventions, and their environmental degradation. Each painting enables us to see the whole in a single moment. The size of each panorama might require our eyes to move across them in order to grasp the details in the entire piece. But stand far enough back and it appears that it's all there at once.

We are seeing the lakes represented visually as we might directly view them from the beach. The paintings show far more detail than we could possibly see at any moment. They depict, as well, prehistory, history, and the present time of the Great Lakes. They are far more complex than any immediate experience might be, but both are visual experiences, initially, of the moment. Rockman's creation of the "Cycle" occurred over several years—over time. It was linear and time-bound as writing is. But my point speaks to the *experience* of the representation. We perceive the paintings visually and at a given moment. They present the all-at-once-ness of the lakes' world. When we write or read, we build a perception over time. Studying a painting or a text moves into different territory, where we are students or scholars rather than simply viewers or readers.

The Grand Rapids Art Museum catalogue for the exhibition explains in detail the sources and influences for Rockman's paintings. He has developed a hybrid artistry that evolves from sources like the 19th-century American Hudson River School (notably Thomas Cole

Alexis Rockman *Cascade*, 2015. Oil and alkyd on wood panel, 72 × 144 inches.
Artists Rights Society (ARS), New York

and Frederick Church), American photorealism, cinema, scientific illustration, and museum dioramas. "Through the careful interlacing of compositional approaches with stylistic languages, pictorial practices, and the vocabularies of science, he made visible crucial narratives that highlight the many stresses on the precarious ecological equilibrium" (Rockman, 45). He tells a visual story. He has made his own mosaic by drawing on several visual vocabularies to present the natural and human past and present of the Great Lakes.

. . .

The paintings include so much detail and information that Rockman provides a key to each image in every painting. "Each picture is packed with centuries of history, dozens of flora and fauna, and thousands of facts" (55). All five paintings are quite wonderful, but "Cascade" simply overwhelms me. It is the first piece he painted. "It was the clearest scene in my mind as I began: just take the lakes and show the many ways they were transformed" (70). "Cascade" portrays life, objects, and activity beneath, on, and above the surface of the water. One can, as the catalogue directs, "read" this visually from left to right. "The story begins with the recession of the Laurentide Ice Sheet" and hunting by Paleo-Indians. Then as one "reads" across it, the painting displays the floral and faunal history of the lakes and its human engagement through time. A small figure of a hunter stands on top of the glacier that over time is shedding ice. This dominates the upper left of the painting. Just below the glacial imagery, three caribou swim thorough the glacial melt that helped create the Great Lakes (70).

The underwater imagery of the piece extends across the lower third, where Rockman traces the evolution of fish from early to modern species, ending on the right with images of damaged or dead, skeletal fish. In the same underwater spaces, Rockman has painted a deteriorating Clovis point and shaft and a Lake Benton pot. Then moving right, he has depicted the wreckage of four lake boats lying on the bottom. Then breaking the surface, the painting displays a small trapper's cabin with very small figures standing in front and a commercial fishing boat with a net extending forward and out of the painting on the lower right. The portrait of the modern industrial world includes images of felled logs floating in the water, iron ore, slag heaps, a Great Lakes bulk carrier, and a coal-driven power plant.

The key that Rockman provides to the painting identifies sixty images. It is the human impact that the painting emphasizes. "Cascade is an allegory of humanity's continuing impact on nature" (70). Its "layered mix of human and natural history draws us in with its dramatic landscape, then its rich range of flora and fauna, and finally, as we delve deeper, the message that individuals, communities and governments must take a long-term view for stewardship of the lakes" (70).

Unless one stands before "Cascade," as I have, it is difficult to convey the wonder it inspires and the way the painting condenses centuries into simultaneous visual imagery which we perceive at one time. It gives us a dramatic, visual sense of the Great Lakes in one large (six-by-twelve-foot) complex painting. The piece achieves some sense of scale, depth, and perspective. It also, as I see it, flattens the imagery somewhat. That suggests a certain simultaneity—as if everything in the painting bears on the present moment. And it is all there at the moment—unlike texts which are much more sequential.

To appreciate fully, however, what we're seeing, we do need to "read" the pictures. We rely on the key and also bring external information and knowledge to them. For all the richness of imagery and representation in "Cascade," and for the remarkable knowledge of the lakes Rockman brings to the "Cycle," not to speak of his artistry, the paintings make a point; they express a theme. They do not include the immediacy of individual or personal experience, or specific details about the society, economy, and culture of the lakes—the experience and knowledge that extended texts provide.

"The Great Lakes Cycle" is truly an extraordinary achievement—ambitious, comprehensive, knowledgeable, artful. Nothing I know compares to it—certainly nothing in the profusion of lake images available in shops and galleries all along Lake Michigan, even considering the most artful work. In the end, however, like every text, the reality of the lakes exceeds even what the "Cycle" achieves. That ultimate limitation relates to the way the lakes—and for me specifically, Lake Michigan—cannot be captured fully in words or images. The lakes cannot be known entirely, historically or scientifically. They cannot be managed or controlled completely by us no matter how expert and talented writers, artists, or scientists might be. I could double the length of this small book yet still not capture it all or turn representation into reality. Compromised and "controlled" to the extent they are, the lakes remain part of the wild.

• 7 •

The Invasive Juggernaut

Beneath the Shimmering, Mesmerizing Surface

Have you ever looked at the maw of a sea lamprey—that vicious, destructive predator? It is "a large, oral sucking disk with sharp, horn-shaped teeth surrounding a razor sharp, rasping tongue" (Fishery Commission). The photos I'm looking at make that maw especially repulsive and threatening. Lampreys grow to fourteen to twenty-four inches. They attach that maw to fish, dig in with their teeth, prey on body fluids, and insert an enzyme that prevents blood clotting. The fish die from the attack or from infection. A single lamprey can kill forty pounds of fish in just over a year. At their peak, they were

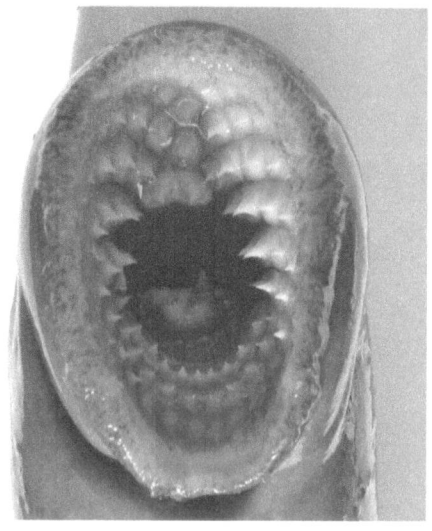

Sea lamprey maw *(Photo by William Rapai)*

destroying more than one hundred million pounds of fish every year—five times the commercial harvest. They caused the fishery to collapse and the economy to decline. A lamprey control program was introduced, which reduced their numbers by 90 percent. The fishery began to recover.

It's time, I know, to move on to other invaders, but I couldn't get that killer out of my mind—a striking image of what lies below the beautiful surface. There is no magic down there—or if so, it's a dark magic or a force that disrupts and destroys.

The story continues with the St. Lawrence Seaway opening in 1959, enabling oceangoing ships to travel from the Atlantic into the Great Lakes—all the way to Duluth, Minnesota. The Seaway promised great economic benefits, and for a time it delivered. The Seaway, however, was not built wide enough to accommodate modern container ships. And then over time, shipping needs and destinations changed. The Seaway's economic value declined sharply. Its destructive effects, however, did not.

The Seaway, like the Welland Canal many years before, exposed the lakes to non-native and destructive species—algae, mollusks, and fish. "They started turning up at a rate never before seen" (Egan, 109). They migrated across the ocean in the ballast water of oceangoing ships which then dumped the water in the Seaway or in the lakes on their way to port. Apparently, in the 1980s, the U.S. sold massive amounts of grain to the Soviet Union. To transport the grain, "an armada of rust-bucket freighters from the Black and Caspian Seas sailed into Great Lakes ports to pick up the precious food" (Rapai, 35). They left behind ballast water and a huge number of non-native organisms—worsening an already bad situation.

Zebra mussels, "an invasive species juggernaut," caused the first problem. The mussels fasten on any hard surface—boats, docks, buoys. They clog water intake pipes. They reproduce in huge numbers. "Each female can produce one million eggs per year" (Egan, 112). Industries and cities have spent millions on chemicals and devices to keep pipes open so that water flows freely to industry, businesses, and residences.

Quagga mussels came next. They've caused even greater damage and trouble. They feast on plankton and effectively consume the base of the lake's food chain and virtually smother the lake bed. Over time, the fish population declined—or "crashed," as some have described it.

The goby fish, yet another invader from the Caspian Sea in the 1990s, spread through all the lakes in just three years. They also reproduce in great numbers. A few years ago, there might have been as many as nine billion gobies in Lake Erie alone. They devour fish eggs and thereby reduce the fish population. They prey on the zebra and quagga mussels, but that hasn't eliminated them. The mussels have cleared the water so that sunlight penetrates more deeply. That enables seaweed to grow on the shells and virtually cover the lake bottom. Occasionally some breaks off, with the mussel shells attached. The decomposition of the seaweed releases a botulism-causing bacteria. Mussels consume the bacteria; they are, in turn, eaten by gobies; paralyzed gobies rise to the surface and become prey for birds; birds then feed on them and die. By one count, from the late 1990s until about 2015, "more than 100,000 loons, grebes, ducks, cormorants, and gulls ... died" (Rapai, 56).

There have been attempts to control the mussels. A toxin, Zequanox, was developed that killed zebras and quaggas, but not other organisms. For various reasons, including the cost of widespread application for one, the toxin will probably not be used widely. There is no "silver bullet" (Rapai, 67).

Not until 1990 did Congress pass legislation to regulate ballast water discharge. The EPA had chosen in 1972 to concentrate on inland water and ignore ballast water discharge and lake pollution. This is a long, complicated, contentious story of inadequate enforcement, ineffective legislation, conflicting interests, and multiple governmental authorities. For my purpose, however, it's enough to say this attempt at human intervention or ecological management seems to have failed. It has led to destructive consequences virtually beyond our control.

The opening of the Seaway and the ballast water releases, e.g., triggered a chain of invasions and events that now are "natural" and perhaps unmanageable. Lake Michigan has changed drastically. As one biologist put it—sad that his children would not know his lake, and certainly not my magical lake: "This isn't the lake it was 25 years ago, and it's probably not the same lake it's going to be in 10 years" (Egan, 130).

• • •

And now the backdoor threat of Asian carp. A species of Asian grass carp was imported and released in Arkansas to clear weeds and seaweed from southern ponds and rivers. That solved one problem. Then later, an Arkansas fish farmer trying to replicate that success mistakenly (or accidentally) imported three other carp species—silver, bighead, and black carp. They were not weed eaters. So the farmer turned them over to the state. The state started a breeding program, assuming these filter-feeding carp could clean up sewage lagoons. The program succeeded only with silver and bigheaded carp, but a lack of funding ended the project. Some carp were then released with no sense they'd do any harm. The fish, presumably, could not breed in the wild—it had been so difficult under controlled conditions. "This was a blunder of the highest order" (Egan, 156).

The carp could, in fact, reproduce, and did in large numbers. They appeared in rivers and streams throughout the south and steadily migrated north. Silver and bigheaded carp feed on plankton—thus the hope that they could filter sewage lagoons. In large numbers, the carp eat the plankton other fish depend on and thereby push out native species. Some estimate that in certain parts of the Mississippi, the carp constitute 90 percent of the biomass. Should they ever colonize Lake Michigan, they could disrupt its fishery and its commercial and sport fishing industries. Once again what began as a solution to a problem—seaweed in rivers and streams—resulted in a serious threat to Lake Michigan.

Some biologists assume that silver and bigheaded carp could not survive in Lake Michigan's open waters, but no one obviously wants to test that. The Army Corps of Engineers has worked on electrified barrier solutions that so far have succeeded. Even though signs of carp DNA have been found north of the barrier, no carp have been seen or caught in the lake. In 2009, there was a big fish-kill in the canal between the lake and the Chicago River. No dead Asian carp floated up anywhere near the lake. As late as 2019, no carp had passed the barrier—insofar as people could tell. Carp DNA, however, has also been found in Lake Calumet just seven miles from Lake Michigan.

A University of Michigan study released in August 2019 overturned any doubt about the carp thriving in the lake or in rivers feeding into it. It indicated that bighead carp, in particular, could fare a lot better than expected in Lake Michigan. "Our study indicates that the carp can survive and grow in much larger areas of the lake than previous studies suggested" (*AP News*). That gave new emphasis to preventing carp migration into the lake. Governors of eight states and the premiers of two provinces have all endorsed a plan to prevent the carp from entering Lake Michigan.

...

The invasions, disruptions, and threats I've been describing are effects or consequences of human action—the canals, the Seaway, seeding non-native fish into the lakes, and so on. A further threat involves the belief of drier, water-challenged regions that the Great Lakes could satisfy their increasing water requirements. Currently, the states and provinces bordering the lakes have imposed limits on who can draw water from them—only places within the lake watersheds. It probably is a fantasy to pipe water all the way to the semi-arid West. The costs would entail billions and billions of dollars. As water there becomes more and more scarce, however, the pressure to "share" water might well increase. People and politicians possess a remarkable capacity to fantasize and believe they could make it come true. The extended drought in the West could increase the pressure.

· · ·

What then must be done? Dan Egan cites three possible solutions for defending and restoring the fishery. Electric and sound barriers in the Chicago River continue to be improved and extended. Biologists have proposed a genetic solution. Carp genes would be manipulated to compromise the reproductive capacity of the carp. Others have proposed a biotic solution. As the native species recover and flourish—lake trout came back impressively when the alewives disappeared—they would then resist new invasions. Every policy and action under consideration "on both sides of the U.S.-Canada border," William Rapai writes, focuses on "prevention, detection, response, and management" (142).

The federal government continues to fund restoration projects. From 2009 through 2017, the Great Lakes Restoration Initiative from the EPA invested over $2 billion to restore habitat and wetlands, to fight invasive species, clean up toxic pollution, reduce toxic runoff, and control Asian carp. Wetland restoration, e.g., helps communities clean water, prevent flooding, and reduce runoff—problems caused by the clearing of wetlands for new residential and commercial construction and by agricultural expansion. In one sense $2 billion or more sounds like a lot, but when I think of the scale, scope, and complexity of restoring these huge inland seas, the investment seems meager.

• 8 •

Water 3

"We can't control the Great Lakes."
Candice Miller

There is no way to restore the Lake Michigan of my memory and imagination—if it ever existed. The lake might be managed now to a new normal and perhaps provide what people seem to want: "good fishing . . . clean water to drink . . . water that's not carrying parasites that [will] make them sick . . . picnic on the shoreline without smelling rotting sewage or dead animals . . . swim and boat . . . without getting bogged down in slimy weeds. They want simple beauty" (Rapai, 154). I don't know. Nor does anybody else. Despite funding, research, time, and commitment, no one really knows what it will take to repair what we have so profoundly damaged. We might well be living an illusion: the grand illusion that humanity can overcome the "pernicious" (Gary Snyder's apt term) way we have treated nature. It's our hubris that makes us believe we can restore what we have allowed to be damaged, even destroyed. Even if some semblance of a healthy lake could be sustained, it will be "a diminished thing," Elizabeth Kolbert concludes about the Great Barrier Reef (110).

As I follow this long story, I see a pattern of problem, solution, problem—usually an unintended consequence that required still another solution. Attempts to balance the lake's ecosystem succeed in one sense but then fail in consequence—or at least are incomplete, if not inadequate. And that suggests to me the lake and its biology exceed our capacity. It remains a natural force which we manage and damage but never quite dominate. At least so far. "As humans, we always want to be in control, but we can't control the Great Lakes ... We changed it, but we didn't necessarily control it" (Egan, 104).

For all of the dark magic below, however, Lake Michigan still provides a fishery that feeds and entertains, water that sustains towns and cities, a waterway that supports shipping and manufacturing, and clean enough water (most of the time) for beach people. It drives the economies of the surrounding states. We have not yet destroyed or saved it. For all that, Lake Michigan retains its beauty and allure—its shimmering, mesmerizing surface.

• 9 •

The Return

"It begins with the lake. It always does for me."
Michigan writer Mae Stier

I left Michigan after twenty years but returned to the lake from time to time, if not every year. Gradually the hold Lake Michigan had on me seemed to fade. I'd overcome my desire to live there since I lived in the Virginia mountains and was trying to make a place there.

In 1990, Barbara and I built a house in a beautiful mountain valley that had been inhabited and farmed for generations. Some neighbors were fifth, even sixth, generation descendants of people who'd come to the area in the early 1800s. I talked with, learned from, and wrote about the place and its people. We were trying to fit in and make a home in a valley where we had no history or family. We moved there initially for its beauty—purely for the aesthetics. During the ten years I lived in Clover Hollow, however, I came to value and respect the history and culture of the local people. I also learned about myself. Instead of being a man always leaving his pasts, I rediscovered my own hometown and college past and how deeply both had shaped me. I tell their story and the story of my transformation in *Hollow and Home*.

My life in Clover Hollow led me to believe I'd escaped the lure of Lake Michigan. How wrong I was. We'd driven from Stratford, Ontario, to Lake Huron. I anticipated nothing more than a pleasant outing. But when I stood on the beach and looked at the lake, I felt a sharp sense of loss and longing. My eyes teared, my nose filled, my throat choked. The sudden rush of emotion simply overwhelmed me. I couldn't control it. "It brings it all back, doesn't it?" my wife asked.

"Yes, it surely does." I'd simply suppressed my deep emotional attachment. Then came the memories of water and waves, sun and rain on the lake, snow, ice, huge cloud banks, spectacular sunsets, driftwood, windrows of small plants, chaff, and litter on the beach, the feeling of sand between my toes, water washing against me, the fresh smells of lake water, the stench of dead fish—my long history with Lake Michigan from the time I was two. The Great Lakes seep through my body, live in my unconscious, hide, and then erupt in emotion, image, and idea. For days and weeks afterward, that rush of feeling was so fresh, so raw. I couldn't sort it out, let alone escape it. All I could say: "I've got to go back, somehow." To what? To the lake? To a presumably finished past? To a new life there? I didn't know. It was just an impulse.

For months afterwards, feelings of loss and longing surged through me and distanced me emotionally from the home and place we were trying to make in Clover Hollow. The lake enchanted, even haunted me. I began to think (because of problems I was having with an early version of *Hollow and Home*) I would not find anything I searched for—no place or community, no self, other than the wandering, unattached self I'd always been, still leaving his pasts behind.

If we decided to go back to Lake Michigan to live, what kind of return would it be? We wouldn't really be going back home because we'd never actually lived at the lake—although we had both lived in Michigan for twenty years. Might we be returning simply to a magic more compelling than the power of the mountains? Or would such a return be just another departure? My feelings might simply mask a fantasy of return and recovery. They might disguise an impulse to flee flux, uncertainty, aging, even death, and find in the beauty of the lake and my memories a still place.

But even that would be illusory. There is no "still" place in living. Nothing is so unchanging—not even the lake itself. As phenomenon or metaphor, it isn't stable or permanent. It rises and falls within a decade. It turns from liquid to ice. It becomes calm and then turbulent within a day. The sands move minute by minute. The color of the water changes hour after hour. Lake temperatures vary. The surface of the lake and the contours of the shore are far more changeable than the ridges and mountains surrounding Clover Hollow, for all the variety there created by light, weather, and seasons. During those months of recollection, I remembered specific days and weeks at Lake Michigan.

...

We returned to the cottage on the lake after the Carlisle reunion in Ohio in the late 1990s. We were renting the house but even so, I felt like I was coming home. It seemed right to be there and this just a few days after a family reunion. You'd think I would have felt my home was there—in Delaware, Ohio—with my past, with familiar houses, schools, buildings, and neighborhoods. They all, however, seemed like photographs in a family album—artifacts of a past but not a present reality. "I [had] left my hometown in almost every sense and [gone] on to a relatively placeless life. I was a man always leaving his pasts and moving on to the next opportunity—typical of American, middle-class culture." It is "an insidious nomadism," said Edward Casey.

It would take a few more years of living in Clover Hollow and writing *Hollow and Home* before I realized and could say, "I'm grounded in Delaware in a way that overcomes the relative placelessness of my life. I've realized my homecoming through memory, research, visits, conversations, reflection, and imagination." Delaware "made me who I am. It sustains me emotionally, imaginatively, and philosophically. I do indeed dwell there."

That reunion summer, however, I focused on the lake as a place of power and satisfaction—a true home. Although I was writing about Clover Hollow and the mountains and our desire to fit in, I soon realized that I would always be a "come-here," even if I was a bridge between the two cultures, as one of the prominent natives said. We were living *in* the mountains, but we were not *of* them. I wondered if Lake Michigan was not the opposite. Although I was not living at the lake, I was nevertheless *of* it. It imposed a powerful presence in its very absence.

• • •

This afternoon is mostly overcast. A brisk wind blows from the southwest. A light surf breaks almost silently on the beach. Just a few days before, huge waves crashed on the sand from a big blow from the northwest. The lake is a dull green—except for occasional bright spots and sparkle when the sun falls on it. Even though the temperature is in the low seventies, I'm comfortable wearing a windbreaker, a little chilly without it. A few people are walking on the beach. A man, a boy, and a young girl are swimming to my right. Several small boats are moving over the water. Others have anchored for fishing. Three Jet Skis roar by. A dozen seagulls stand at the water's edge to my left.

• • •

We returned to the lake just a year later. On the first day, I felt deeply dispirited. Even the lake could not break my melancholy or soften my anxiety. By the second day, I felt more settled and at home—calmer and more peaceful. The lake was having its way. The weather was warm and humid the first week. By late afternoon the house heated up, but we didn't feel uncomfortable sitting on the terrace or walking along the beach. After sunset, cool air flowed through the house, and we slept well.

After two days in DC for a wedding, we gladly came back to Lake Michigan, where I felt settled, if not calm and serene: in harmony with the lake, with the rhythms of the surf, its flowing and ebbing, the gentle slap of calm water on the beach, the rush and crash of big waves, the changing horizon line—blurred one day by a humid haze, razor sharp after a front passed. I didn't feel the deep longing that had overwhelmed me the year before. I felt that I belonged there—although the actuality of ever living at the lake still seemed remote, not so much a fantasy, just remote.

...

Two freighters came in today—one this morning from the Medusa Cement Company, the other late in the afternoon, the James Norris of the Upper Lakes Ltd., flying a Canadian flag. The house we're in sits on the north shore of Grand Haven, just above the harbor opening. I watched the Norris come in from the lake, pause outside the channel entrance, and then sail on in. And so, I pause and think, again, about living here. I know the contentment I'm feeling might not last beyond the moment, then would come the ache of failure, the anxiety of trying over and over, the burdens of keeping up with my academic work and all the demands of our mountain house and land. I am not tired of that life, yet—but the lake, the lake, the lake. Its magic and majesty slowly enfold me. I know I will come back, if only for a few weeks each year until . . . ?

A front passed through last night. We've had a strong blow all day out of the northwest. The surf is up. Five- and six-foot waves break across the pier, flooding the cement surface and soaking me as I stand with my camera, shooting waves and surfers. The flags at the lakeside houses ripple and crack in the steady blow and point sharply southeast. Earlier this morning, I watched the steady flow of waves coming in from the northwest, but then noticed an occasional "across the grain" wave action. Waves collided and broke high in a white spray and foam—like water breaking on the beach.

Late in the day—it's 7:45 now—the lake is a deep olive green, broken by whitecaps and the rolling surface. The sun, now low in the sky, shines through the whitecaps, making them translucent—now a pattern of olive green, translucent edges, shadows under the waves turning over, white crests, and then it all breaks up on the beach. The setting sun creates a wide, brilliant river of reflected light—too intense to look at directly. It gives the waving dune grass a silver sheen in contrast with its flat green. As it has for three straight nights, the sun, a red-orange disc, settles slowly and silently into the lake. There are few clouds—no diffused color, just the red disc.

• 10 •

The Lake Effect

"Water's my will / and my way."
Theodore Roethke

Late in the summer of my Huron moment, I described for friends what I'd felt at the Huron shore the day Barbara and I drove there from Stratford. As I talked, my eyes teared again, my throat caught . . . And there I was, in a home, on a Virginia mountainside, longing for water—for Lake Michigan. I talked about my childhood experiences and the lifelong attachment to the lake they'd inspired. I told them about the pleasures and satisfactions of staying at the lake.

I described Lake Michigan in summer and winter: the sparkle of sunlight on the water; the muted light of overcast days; the water's blue or green or leaden color, depending on light and time of day; whitecaps as waves broke offshore, waves spilling or crashing on the sand, the easy, quiet swells on calm days; the hot sand, sharp dune grass, and small beech trees along the front dune; and the snow and ice building up on the beach. My rhapsody could have gone on and on. I wanted them to understand the emotional power of the lake and how deeply—and irrationally—I identified with it.

Barbara and I had been spending a week or two each December on the Captivas—islands off the Florida Gulf coast. "Could the Captivas give you the same water and beach magic you experience at Lake Michigan?" my friends asked. "Not at all," I replied. "I enjoy the islands—especially the remoteness of North Captiva. It's accessible only by boat."

A 1921 hurricane ripped North Captiva from Captiva and created Red Fish Pass. There are residences, a beach club with a pool, and an airstrip, but no cars. Undeveloped state land covers the south part of the island. People get around by golf cart, bicycle, or on foot. There were two modest restaurants and one very small food store on the island. We would book a water taxi from Pine Island and would carry with us all the food and other supplies we needed. If we ran out or forgot something, we could order small quantities of groceries through the store that would come the next day.

One year, we'd rented a cottage at the north end of the island looking across Captiva Pass to Cayo Costa. As I was standing at the water's edge one warm evening, the sun was setting into the gulf, on my left, just as a full moon was rising over Pine Island Sound on my right. A red sun and a brilliant white moon. Remarkable. For all its appeal, I explained to my friends, "North Captiva is no more than a great vacation place. But I have no history, no family attachments, no emotional connection other than the pleasure of being on a lovely Gulf Coast island in December." My Lake Michigan passion is too deep, too complex, for anything to replace or substitute for it. The lake simply lives within me.

Weeks had passed between the Huron moment and our conversation. Life had taken over. I'd been attending not only to my work at Virginia Tech, but also to our new home and the eighty acres of mountainside that surrounded it. I knew how blessed I was to live in the midst of such beauty and near generous and considerate neighbors, many of whose families had lived in the valley for generations. Nevertheless, the lake was always there, silently calling.

• • •

Our neighbors in Clover Hollow had welcomed us into the community as valued "come-heres" trying to find a way to fit in. We started by building a house that paid homage to the local farmhouse architecture but also included contemporary variations on that traditional style. Important as that gesture was, I also felt a strong desire to learn as much as I could about our neighbors and their ancestors and about Clover Hollow. And I did. I wrote essays and then a book. Clover Hollow became a site of discovery for me and transformed my sense of self, place, and past.

In the end, however, I realized my deepest roots could not in fact be there. I was and would always be a "come-here," no matter how valued I might be. I was living *in* the place—even somewhat embedded in it—but I would never be *of* it. So once again, as I had throughout my adult life, I left Clover Hollow and moved on—not toward "my" Lake Michigan, but even further south. I was swept along in a current of life somewhat out of my control—swept away to South Florida on the Atlantic coast.

...

I lived in Lake Worth Beach with my late wife, Barbara, for six years, and then for a few more after her death in 2007. The town was settled originally in the late 19th century and incorporated as the town of Lake Worth in 1913. It was named for the large, once freshwater lake between the mainland and the Palm Beach barrier island. The intracoastal waterway now travels through it. The city benefited from the 1920s land boom in Florida. A bridge across the lagoon was built in 1919. The casino and a beach complex on the island opened shortly after.

The architecture of the older downtown buildings is primarily Moorish, and many of the buildings date from the 1920s. A former school from the 1920s now houses the City Hall Annex. The main City Hall occupies what was originally a WPA gymnasium. The Gulfstream Hotel, with an elegant lobby and dining room, is also from the 1920s. The National Register of Historic Places lists it, but unfortunately, it has been closed for years.

By the 1980s and '90s, the town had deteriorated, with a rising crime rate and declining buildings. Lake Worth Beach, however, was recovering when we first visited. We purchased, renovated, and expanded a 1947 bungalow on a street where the oldest houses dated from the 1920s. It faced the intracoastal waterway across a golf course. Our architect designed an exceptional house—artful, comfortable, even seductive, as one potential buyer suggested. It satisfied in many ways.

We lived near water. We could see the Intracoastal and the Palm Beach barrier island. We could walk to the Atlantic in twenty minutes, drive in five. For six months we swam at the beach every Wednesday and Sunday morning—a satisfying ritual at the time. Then came Barbara's ovarian cancer diagnosis. Everything changed.

• • •

In recent decades, the city's downtown has been booming with art galleries, shops, restaurants, and bars. The residential areas in the east part of town have developed attractively. The downtown seems like a real one—unlike developments that have built a commercial and restaurant area along a major artery and called it "downtown." Lake Worth Beach feels like an older Florida. It has largely escaped the artifice and extravagance of the new, highly developed, and wealthy South Florida. But that world surrounds the city and presses in upon it.

The city and my residence captured the Florida dilemma. The state is serious yet bizarre, familiar yet strange, settled yet constantly changing, honest yet corrupt, modest yet extravagant, economically marginal yet an absurdly wealthy Disneyland or Dubai-like state. It never felt quite like a real place and certainly not home in the deep sense, even though my wife, Beth, whom I married in 2010, and I spent several winters in Lake Worth Beach and then in Palm Beach Gardens—dividing our time between Florida and her family farm in the Virginia mountains. In the end, we moved full time to the farm and treated Florida merely as a winter escape—as North Captiva had been for me years before—and the Atlantic as a vast, saltwater ocean, impressive and sometimes overwhelming, but still not an equivalent to the sweet-water Great Lakes.

• 11 •

Water 4

"*Unpredictable, Massive, and Unforgiving*"
Matt Stofsky

The SS *Carl D. Bradley* set sail on November 18, 1958, for her home port in Rogers City, Michigan. The ship had just delivered a load of crushed stone to Gary, Indiana. Winds of twenty-five-to-thirty-five miles per hour were blowing when she departed. The course was taking her toward a storm of high seas and gale-force winds—sixty-to-sixty-five miles per hour. For the first part of the trip, Captain Bryan, known as a "heavy weather" captain, sailed close to the Wisconsin shore for protection. Then, he made the turn for home near Beaver Island. Late the next day, he reported that the ship "was riding comfortably with a heavy following sea."

The crew enjoyed a 4:00 p.m. dinner of hamburgers and french fries. At 5:28, "a loud thud resounded through the ship." In the pilothouse, the captain and the first mate "stared in horror as the ship's stern appeared to sag." The hull cracked, broke in two, and began to sink. The first mate sent a mayday. "Mayday! Mayday! Mayday! This is the *Carl D. Bradley*; our position is approximately twelve miles southwest of Gull Island. We are in serious trouble. We're breaking up." The captain ordered, "Abandon ship." But the men in the stern could not lower the lifeboats. Four crewmen in the bow did reach a life raft as the bow sank, but only two survived being thrown off the raft over and over by massive waves. The ship exploded as it sank.

It went down in water 350 feet deep far out in the lake (*Wikipedia* and Great Lakes Shipwreck Museum display text).

High seas made rescue very difficult. A nearby ship that observed the sinking and explosion required an hour and a half to get to the site. Two thirty-six-foot rescue boats from the mainland had to turn back. The Coast Guard cutter *Sundew* from Charlevoix took five hours to reach the search area. It did not find the raft until 8:37 a.m.—fifteen hours after the *Bradley* sank. During the day after, the *Sundew* and other vessels simply collected bodies—seventeen, all wearing life jackets. Of the thirty-five crew members aboard the *Bradley*, only the two on the life raft survived. Thirty-three died. Fifteen bodies were never recovered.

For twenty-two years, the SS *Carl D. Bradley* was the largest ship on the Great Lakes, at 639 feet. An icebreaker as well as a freighter, the *Bradley* usually sailed first through the Straits of Mackinac at the spring thaw. It was the costliest shipwreck in Great Lakes history.

• • •

My cousin Carol Lucas took the telephone call from Bradley Transportation in Rogers City the night the ship sank. The company was calling her father, Robert H. Lucas, to tell him the ship had gone down. When my Uncle Bob was the chief engineer with Michigan Limestone in Rogers City, the *Bradley* sailed for the company. He probably knew the ship's officers, as well as some of its crew. Besides noting the loss professionally, he must have grieved for the thirty-three dead sailors.

The *Bradley* was the company's jewel. She was known as "The Queen of the Lakes." The boat provided handsome guest staterooms and often carried corporate officials and their guests. During a family visit one summer, my uncle hosted us for lunch on the *Bradley* while it was in port. He occasionally treated his own family for lunch on the ship. He also arranged a weeklong Great Lakes *Bradley* cruise for my mother and their sister Isabel. Carol traveled with them that summer. During college, David Lucas, Carol's brother, worked three summers on the boats. As one of the lowest level workers, he was assigned jobs in the engine room, on deck moving equipment and painting, and in the kitchen washing dishes and serving tables. The engine room demanded the most. "When we shoveled coal . . . had to wipe surfaces and sweep the floor to keep the engine room as clean as possible . . . There was a lot of smoke in the air," Lucas said. They worked seven days a week, on four-hour shifts with breaks, and with one long eight-hour break.

The Rogers City limestone quarry, now known as Calcite, is the largest in the world. It began production in 1912. By 1929 the company was quarrying eleven million tons of stone a year. It supplied most of the limestone for the steel industry in the Great Lakes region. Bradley Transportation boats carried most of that to mills in the lower lakes. The cargo of one freighter can carry the loads of as many as three thousand trucks. Overall, Great Lakes shipping saves $350 billion each year in land transportation costs. It's obviously a very economical way of transporting limestone, as well as iron ore.

SS *Carl D. Bradley* *(Courtesy of Historical Collections of the Great Lakes, Bowling Green State University)*

Calcite continues as a major supplier for the steel industry. It now loads as many as three hundred freighters annually.

...

A weeklong trip to the Upper Peninsula distilled for me the economic and social effects of Great Lakes shipping. We crossed Mighty Mac, the five-mile bridge to the Upper Peninsula, and headed for Sault Ste. Marie—the "Soo." I had not been there in years; Beth had never been. The house we leased faced the St. Mary's River—the channel the freighters travel going up or down between Lake Superior and Lakes Michigan and Huron. We watched freighters travel by in the morning mist, lit mysteriously after dark, and in the bright light of midday. The boats passed quietly. Only the faint rumble of the engines broke the silence.

The *Algoma Equinox* passed early one morning. One of three relatively new ships owned by the Canadian Steamship lines, it carries mostly iron ore and grain. It sails the Great Lakes and the St. Lawrence Seaway. We would see it again later in the day when we were touring the Soo locks.

The tour boat we'd booked entered the MacArthur lock; the partly-wooden gates closed slowly behind us; we sat quietly for a moment, enclosed within the lock's high walls; the boat then slowly rose twenty-one feet to the level of Lake Superior; at the same time, a freighter was being lowered in the adjacent Poe Lock. From the deck of our small boat, that one seemed immense. At the top, the gates opened, and we moved into the wide St. Marys River. Later, as the tour boat headed back for our descent, the *Algoma Equinox* was leaving the Poe Lock on its way to Lake Superior.

The sight of the boats on the river and the one in the Poe Lock opened for me a world of information and reflection about the lakes' effects economically and socially. The Soo Locks control all shipping that moves between Lake Superior and the other lakes. Boats make as many as ten thousand passages through the locks annually. Were they ever closed, the economic effects would be profound.

- 100 percent of North American auto production would halt within weeks of shutdown.
- In thirty days, a shutdown of the Soo Locks would create a $160 million economic impact.
- A six-month shutdown of the Soo Locks would result in eleven million jobs lost nationwide.
- 100 percent of the iron ore mined in the U.S. comes through the Soo Locks.
- $500.4 billion worth of iron ore passes through the locks annually.
- The Soo Locks handle seventy-five million tons of commerce annually.

The Soo also attracts as many as half a million visitors each year. Even though tourism contributes only 6 percent to the overall economy of Sault Ste. Marie, the $164.4 million visitors spent in a recent year significantly supported businesses, restaurants, and hotels. The locks benefit the Soo socially, as well as economically, by attracting all these visitors.

• • •

I'm dwelling momentarily on Great Lakes shipping—and water—because of my family connections, as well as my interest in every facet, function, image, and meaning of Lake Michigan. My family's lunch on the *Bradley*, my mother's tour, the Lucas family's experience in Rogers City, my cousin crewing summers on freighters, Robert Lucas's professional life in shipping, the SS *Bradley* as part of the fleet at Michigan Limestone when he worked there, the violent storm that sank her, my grandfather as a mill superintendent at the U.S. Steel Gary Works, the *Bradley's* port of departure —it is all intertwined.

From this perspective, the SS *Bradley* serves as a kind of symbol or metonym. The ship sailed the lakes for decades. It can represent, therefore, all lake shipping and its place in the economy. But more than that, the *Bradley's* life and fate speak to the lake's power and beauty and to the beneficial and tragic ways it affects people. It reveals water as both a partner, in economic and social terms, and an existential "adversary," in Bachelard's terms, a force to confront and overcome.

Even in more modern times, with greater safety provisions, stronger and larger ships, and sophisticated guidance systems, "Great Lakes Commerce remains a dangerous business; the lakes are unpredictable, massive, and unforgiving" (Stofsky). Lake Michigan remains a powerful force. It is still part of the unconquered wild.

• 12 •

The Gold Coast: Tourism, Affluence, and the Others

"Past and present jumble together here, some parts planned, other parts wild as the wind."

Michigan Guidebook

"Goodness," Beth said, as she gazed in wonder from the top of a four-hundred-foot-high sand dune. The boats and people along the beach looked almost like toys; they were so far away, she observed. Then she looked out at the vast expanse of Lake Michigan. I see her now standing at the top of that dune. She is wearing a brimmed straw hat and sunglasses, one hand securing her hat against the wind—the deep blue of Lake Michigan and the lighter blue of the cloudless sky in the distance behind her.

I was introducing Beth to "my" Michigan where I'd lived for twenty years, and to northern Michigan and the lake, where I'd spent many days and weeks, many months in effect, over the decades. We were traveling a bit like tourists. We were also exploring the aesthetic, emotional, social, economic, and cultural effects, as well as the natural power, of Lake Michigan. And we'd be traveling beyond the dynamic present into history. We'd do so directly and personally rather than analytically or conceptually, as academics typically do. That has been my point throughout: to discover and express these abstractions as we live them, *in situ*.

Beth on the dune near Pierce Stocking Drive

In my experience, the moment and its meaning are fully intertwined. The analytical, or abstract, emerges from personal experience. And once that has been asserted, personal experience gives it meaning in the world. Each reveals and gives meaning to the other. From a lived perspective, I am suggesting a wholeness to our immediate experiences and our interpretation of them. There is movement or flow that makes conceptually distinct entities inseparable. I am still trying to write from the oppositional perspective I've explained earlier, and at the same time insist on the wholeness in the oppositional achieved through movement and flow.

• • •

On this 2018 trip, my Virginia farm girl discovered a world like none she'd ever known. I felt, once again, the magic of the lake and recalled so many moments from my long history with it. Every time I go, I learn something new and experience the lake differently. It changes, but it doesn't. I see it differently, but then I don't. As a quasi-tourist,

I enjoyed every moment and all the aesthetic, psychological, and historical satisfactions of touring. At the same time, I thought about what each place meant economically and socially. I couldn't attend just to the charm of the lake and the affluence it enables. There is so much more—"the rest," as I think of it. I end up both telling a story and explaining almost simultaneously.

...

On that trip, we stayed in a Traverse City condo near downtown. Our time fell between the National Cherry Festival, celebrated every summer since 1925, and the Traverse City Film Festival, cofounded by Michael Moore in 2005. The cherry festival celebrates the cherry industry. It draws half a million people over its eight days. The film festival is committed to the idea that "One Great Movie Can Change You: Just Great Movies." In 2019, the festival exhibited 194 films at several venues. Thousands of film lovers attend this every summer. During our in-between week, however, sidewalks were less crowded, shops and art galleries comfortably available. Most restaurants could seat us. The lines at the food-truck court at the edge of the downtown weren't so long. It was a normal summer for the city and the nearby resorts.

Then came the pandemic. It forced cancellation of the 2020 Cherry Festival, and it limited the 2021 program offerings: no air show, no arts and crafts fair, no big musical events—no massive events at all. Fewer than the usual half a million attended. The people that did, and those who worked the festival, risked greater exposure to covid. Directly after the event, the county health department announced extended hours for testing—assuming perhaps an increased rate of infection. Both the 2020 and 2021 film festivals were cancelled at a noticeable economic cost.

Even so, in 2021, tourism in Traverse City seemed to explode as people everywhere felt liberated from pandemic restrictions. Downtown sidewalks were jammed. The streets clogged with traffic. Shops and restaurants were all busy. You could tell from the casual, even careless way many dressed that most were not among the summer or year-round affluent. But assuredly, most were White. I smiled at myself—unable on those streets to bask in the charm of the affluent Gold Coast. I smile now at my presumption in judging how other people dress or look.

...

The main part of Traverse City lies at the southern end of the West Bay of Grand Traverse Bay. The Leelanau Peninsula, west of the city, separates the bay from Lake Michigan. The Old Mission Peninsula, a relatively narrow strip running south to north, divides Grand Traverse Bay into the West and East Bays. The mouth of the bay opens to the north into the big lake, where it is twelve miles wide. There are many small inland lakes throughout the area, as well—Crystal, Glen, Leelanau, Little Traverse, Elk, and Torch. Some, like Lake Charlevoix, open directly into Lake Michigan.

The west shore of the state, from Saugatuck on north, is lined by similar lakes, many with channels opening into the big lake. The old cottage on White Lake where I stayed many years ago overlooked the channel connecting White Lake with Lake Michigan. In Grand Haven, a favorite beach town, the Grand River serves as a channel between Spring Lake and the big lake.

The Traverse City area has been known to Europeans since the 1600s, when French explorers and fur traders passed through and reported the difficult passage across the bay's mouth as being *la grande traversée*. For centuries before the whites came, Native Americans made that same passage and also canoed along the Lake Michigan shore from Mackinac Island to Grand Traverse Bay—traveling to and from summer hunting grounds. The Algonquin people had inhabited the area since 900 AD, centuries before the French appeared.

The city and northwest Michigan began developing into its present form in the late 19th century as a summer escape from Chicago and Detroit. People traveled by train and lake steamer to this Gold Coast and to their summer cottages and mansions on the mainland or on Mackinac Island. In 1871, the steamer *City of Traverse* began regular Chicago-Traverse City runs. The Manitou steamed from Chicago to Harbor Springs. And in 1872, the Grand Rapids and Indiana Railroad began service. Its lines reached Mackinaw City in 1882. The Chicago and Western Michigan Railway also brought service to Traverse City in 1892. The area was becoming a major summer resort for people from the Midwest.

The Grand Hotel opened in 1887 to serve those coming north by steamboat or railroad. It continues to this day as the grande dame of Mackinac Island and northern Michigan luxury. It is the largest summer hotel in the world, and it enjoys the longest front porch anywhere—660 feet. It boasts magnificent accommodations. Most room costs for July 2022 ranged from roughly $900 to as much as $1,899 per night, depending on the size and view. It serves as a symbol of luxury, as well as being an active hotel.

For a moment, I imagine myself traveling by sail or rail to my summer home on the Leelanau Peninsula, or in Harbor Springs, or to my "cottage" or Grand Hotel accommodation on the island. Then I drift to the present and sail north on my yacht, fly on my jet, or drive my Corvette or Bentley. The appeal of that gilded glamour disappears when I look out the window of our small Chevrolet rental car. We're driving through inland Michigan on Route 115, past Cadillac, toward Traverse City. We're passing through ordinary rural America—corn and hayfields this time of year, a few large farms with neatly painted barns and outbuildings, other barns with paint flaking, some unused, even collapsing, small houses with pickups beside them, roadside service stations, and a few local highway restaurants. I live closer to this world and doubtless to the tourists crowding Traverse City than to the luxuries of northern Michigan and Mackinac Island. I can fantasize but also observe and think.

For all its pretension, the Grand Hotel has entered the world of tourists. We can pay ten dollars to see its lobbies, sit on its front porch, or enjoy lunch in the dining room facing the straits. Seated at a table on that grand front porch, Beth conducted a Zoom meeting of her Virginia League of Women Voters organization. At one point and with a smile, she turned her computer to show the attendees the view over the Straits of Mackinac. I sat in a nearby rocker and with a sense of irony watched Beth sign on to the hotel's internet and run her meeting. Our ten-dollar fee reduced the cost of our four-course lunch from fifty dollars to forty dollars. This is as close as we would get to the wealthy's summer world.

• • •

From Beth's sand-dune perch in 2018, she discovered a series of wonders. "Goodness," she would often say when impressed by something new. That northern Michigan served as a major summer resort surprised her. Save for those living in the Great Lakes states and provinces, these remarkable inland seas often do seem remote and undefined—a faraway someplace. Lake Michigan and the sand dunes, however, remained the real wonder. The dune we were standing on rises so steeply from the lake that people must climb up from the beach mostly on all fours. A sign at the top warns the adventurous how long, as in hours, it might take to come back up should they foolishly slide down to the lake. The sign adds, in effect, "And we won't help you if you end up stranded."

The beginnings of these magnificent dunes were formed by sand and gravel pushed there during several glacial periods that started roughly fourteen thousand years ago and ended ten thousand to twelve thousand years ago. Over these years the glaciers carved out the basins for the Great Lakes. The glacial meltwater filled the basins. This geologic action also created perched dunes formed by glacial sands left high above the lake on plateaus. Then over thousands of years, prevailing westerly winds blew the fine sand that continued to build these massive dunes.

We'd driven there along the Pierce Stocking Scenic Drive, a 7.4-mile loop, that climbs on a curving, up-and-down road through beautiful, wooded dunes to the top. The drive was named for a local lumberman who planned, built, and then operated the drive from its opening in 1967 until his death in 1976. I enjoy driving through dune woods, but I love walking in them. There is a quiet beauty in the patterns of light and shadow and the sunlight striking some leaves and not others, and the breeze gently rippling through the trees swaying the sharp dune grass.

We drove back down and then stopped further on at the actual Sleeping Bear Dune. Beth left the car to climb to the top. Halfway up she realized how hard going there would be. She turned around and came back. Once at the top—I've climbed the dune in the past—you can see Lake Michigan in the distance. It appears you could walk there rather easily. But in fact, it is a long, difficult hike through soft sand, up and down a series of dunes.

The Ojibwe legend tells an intriguing story about Sleeping Bear. Fleeing a forest fire on the lake's west shore, a mother bear and two cubs tried to swim across the lake to safety. The mother bear reached shore and waited for her cubs on a high bluff. They foundered and drowned. The mother, however, stayed and waited. The Great Spirit, in honor of her devotion, created the two Manitou Islands, just offshore, in commemoration of her cubs. Wind eventually buried the sleeping mother in sand—the sleeping bear—"where she waits to this day."

The Sleeping Bear National Lakeshore was established by Congress in 1970 "to preserve outstanding natural features including forests, beaches, dunes, and ancient glacial phenomena along 100 km (64 miles) of Lake Michigan shoreline, in order to perpetuate the natural setting for the benefit and enjoyment of the public, and to protect it from developments and inappropriate uses that would destroy its scenic beauty, scientific and recreational value" (*Leelanau.com*). The park encompasses more than seventy-one thousand acres. It includes two villages, Empire and Glen Arbor; North and South Manitou islands; and extensive farm and undeveloped land currently occupied by former owners. Large parts of the park have been designated wilderness areas to keep some sense of the wild. But campers, hikers, and bikers use these areas extensively.

Many property owners strongly—even bitterly—opposed the lakeshore. The park would acquire more than 1,400 tracts of private land. That displacement alone was problematic, but then "a heavy-handed, poorly planned land acquisition program reinforced the bitterness" (National Park Service). It was a classic public and private conflict—a three-sided encounter, really, involving the government's environmental concerns, private property rights, and future housing and golf course development.

The park does protect lakeshore and dunes; it provides extensive outdoor recreation; it benefits the area economically, as well. The National Park Service reported that in 2016 it generated $231 million from tourism. Not all is well, however. The Park Service has identified serious environmental problems. "There are acute and catastrophic impacts, as well as creeping and accumulative problems, from the introduction of exotic plants, insects, diseases, and animals that the native species cannot fight. Increases in nearby development, traffic, and human use affect air and water quality." Once again, a real benefit also causes serious problems.

. . .

Beth might have expected the lake to be just "a lake." But as German friends once observed, "You can't see across it,"—another of the wonders she discovered. I've always known that—although from my grandparents' beach, we could see Chicago, if barely, across the southern edge of the lake. But that was hardly the whole lake, which is well over one hundred miles wide. Not until Ludwig and Brigitta's remark did I realize how striking that fact is.

We were touring the area with Steve and Julie, old friends from lower Michigan who'd moved north to Empire. Steve knows well the history of agriculture and its supporting structures. As a business and a hobby, he restores old barns, and showed us several in the area. This part of the adventure exposed Beth to the agriculture economy of the region. As a farm girl and now the lead partner for three family farms in Virginia, she was charmed by rural northern Michigan—the old farms, barns, and cherry orchards.

We were shopping one morning in the Traverse City farmers' market, where Beth thought, at first, the boxes and boxes of large, dark-red tart cherries were cherry tomatoes. She'd not seen such large cherries before. Stall after stall was selling them. Throughout the area outside the city, orchards were blooming beautifully. Sweet red cherries and the dark, tart ones ripen in July. I still order Montmorency cherry juice concentrate and dried tart cherries from King Orchards on the Leelanau Peninsula.

It is a substantial industry. The first commercial cherry orchard, Ridgewood Farm, was planted in 1893. The climate and soils of the area suit cherry and other fruit production well. The lake moderates the winter temperatures. The snowpack keeps the ground from freezing deeply. The rolling hills and sandy soil of the area allow drainage and good air flow. Michigan produces 70-75 percent of the nation's tart cherries on thirty-six thousand acres of cherry trees. It is among the top four states in sweet cherry production. I sensed something of the scale of production years ago during a tour of a processing plant. I'd never been inside a freezer large enough for trucks. Nor had I ever seen a large dump truck filled with cherry pits.

Steve showed us several barns—one large, beautiful, and very red. My photo captures it in bright sunlight. It sits in an open, well-mowed field. The sunlight has turned the metal roof silver and has sharpened the contrast between the red sides exposed to the sun and the dark, almost black, shaded sides. A bright, cloudless blue sky in the background sets off the barn perfectly. The current owners might use it for storage, rather than as a barn for a farm. It now exists as an aesthetic object and also a sign of significant economic change.

At a weathered, gray barn Steve had worked on, he explained the main structure and support system and how he'd restored the interior. The geometry of the posts and rafters and the variety of grays and browns in the wood gave the interior a remarkable, rustic beauty. Outside the barn, Steve asked us to look closely at the hinges and wood of an external door as he explained how he fixed it so that it works. This barn no longer functions as part of a farm economy, but now has only aesthetic and historical purpose.

Beth felt right at home in these rural places. The agriculture economy is not large, but vegetable, fruit, and wine grapes together make it significant. Farmers still grow corn and gather hay for cattle. Truck farms provide produce and other commodities for in-town farmers' markets. Nevertheless, the Grand Traverse Bay area is listed as one of the most endangered agricultural regions in the United States. The lakes, the scenic land, and the climate make it a highly attractive area for new residents, vacation homes, and the golf courses summer residents require. The two economic forces conflict. The red barn and Steve's restored barn were telling me that.

Even the cherry industry has suffered worrisome losses. Crop failures partly explain recent declines. The industry experienced two seasons of dramatically reduced production—less than half each year of the 2019 production. Some farms, however, have seen declining production for a decade. "Increasingly erratic weather is a huge problem—evidence that the climate crisis is hurting the industry" (Interlochen Public Radio). These recent failures might be a matter of bad luck. They also reflect the effects of climate change. As this is "felt globally, Michigan farmers are experiencing it firsthand." Some experts foresee long-term decline. "Agriculture economist Bill Knudson said Michigan's tart industry may be gone in 10 years . . . That would mean a significant economic and cultural change to northern Michigan" (Interlochen). I don't know whether development pressure has contributed to the losses, but they figure into part of the overall decline of agriculture and into an uncertain economic and cultural future.

...

There has been resistance to the loss. The Grand Traverse Regional Land Conservancy, e.g., has acted to protect farmland. During its recently completed $71 million Campaign for Generations, the conservancy placed seventeen farms and a total of more than 7,500 acres under conservation easement—a designation that prevents any future, large-scale residential development. According to the conservancy, nearly ninety projects were completed as part of this effort, including more than twenty new nature preserves, parks and natural areas. In addition, more than thirty new miles of trail were built. Through 2018, the GTRLC had protected more than forty-one thousand acres of land and 125 miles of shoreline.

The conservancy explains: "The very reasons why people love this area could disappear unless we act now to conserve the lands that are most important for water quality, food production, scenic beauty, wildlife habitat, outdoor recreation and community connections. The need to come together to protect our most important land and water resources has never been more urgent."

This kind of news impressed Beth. She was the founding executive director of the New River Land Trust in Virginia. During her seven-year leadership, the NRLT placed forty thousand acres of farmland under easement and preserved miles along the New River. Land conservancy work helps balance preservation with development—a constant tension. The Dow Foundation, a major donor to the Grand Traverse group, values that balance: "Ongoing growth comes with the potential to ruin much of what makes the region so special . . . the Conservancy is in an excellent position to help achieve that balance going forward."

...

Real estate has been booming in recent years, especially in luxury housing—and this despite the pandemic. Homebuilders in northern Michigan are swamped with work, according to an August 2020 news report. Some are booked two years ahead and not taking on new clients. "I have never seen such a rate of booming real estate in 30 years of my professional career," said a Harbor Springs realtor. In Petoskey and Harbor Springs, e.g., the average sale price that year was more than double the statewide average. As late as December 26, 2021, the *Traverse City Record-Eagle* reported that "the real estate buying frenzy remains in full force." The pressure to convert farmland to housing development seems to increase yearly. This boom masks in some sense the housing shortage that exists as a result, especially for employees and people not part of the affluent classes.

A few years later, the drive from Suttons Bay to Northport and beyond reinforced my sense of change. The road passes along the bay in several places. It's a beautiful drive. It also passes by abandoned house trailers, a barnyard filled with junk appliances, barns with rusting metal roofs, some unused, a few collapsing. Modest residential development has occurred where the road runs close to the bay, but I saw mainly agricultural decline. We did pass an herb farm and a few vineyards, but we also drove by many open, fallow fields, some with scrub vegetation taking over. The wild was beginning to come back.

The road through the middle of the Leelanau shows a similar landscape—orchards, vineyards, and corn and hay fields, but many fallow ones as well, and barns with faded and chipped paint and rusting roofs, some no longer in use. The active farms support the general economy, but that world is obviously quite distinct from the tourist crowds and Gold Coast affluence. Even so, these different worlds or cultures are clearly interdependent.

We were headed toward a cottage beyond Northport. Our friends Blaine and Mardi knew the owners and hoped they'd find someone at home. They walked around the house and knocked on the door, but no one was there. In the brief time we were, I had a Blue Mind moment. I walked a short way to the bay's edge, looked out, and felt all my hidden tension flow away—down from my neck, through my shoulders, my chest and belly, descending through my legs, and then out and away. The sight and sounds of the vast expanse of water gave me a moment of total relaxation and peace. The feeling lasted only minutes, its effect much longer. The contrast of the peace inspired by water and my sense of agricultural decline suggest how the glow of the Gold Coast and the lake could easily become the glare of change and loss.

• • •

During the 2018 trip, we reserved a table at Trattoria Stella on 11th Street in Traverse City. Unsure of its location, we relied on our GPS—which to my surprise led us away from downtown, through residential areas, and finally to what obviously had been a mental institution. The architecture of the buildings was unmistakable—especially the Victorian-Italianate style of the main building with its several towers. The Northern Michigan Asylum was established in 1881 and opened to patients in 1885. Over time, it had several names—the last: Traverse City State Hospital. At one time it was the largest employer in the area. The main building—there's a postcard picture of it on the web—was listed on the National Register of Historic Places in 1978 and designated a Michigan State Historic Site in 1985. After several transformations, the hospital closed in 1989.

Eventually, developers converted the main buildings into condominiums, shops, restaurants, and business offices. It is now The Village at Grand Traverse Commons. The old asylum has become part of northern Michigan's affluent and tourist world—part of the Gold Coast. That was a discovery, even for me.

On our way into Stella another time, we talked with one of the condo residents. He'd volunteered to assist with watering the flower gardens throughout the complex. We met him at a circular garden in the center of the parking lot outside the restaurant. "I've lived here several years," he said, "and like it very much. It feels like a real community. By volunteering, as many of us do, we contribute to that." He lives there year-round—no escapes to warmer winter climates. In him I recognized the total transformation of a once-upon-a-time mental institution. He was the rational, human face of affluent and adaptive reuse.

...

Besides enabling the cherry, apple, and peach industry, the lake-effect climate also has produced a considerable wine industry. The Grand Traverse region has two of Michigan's four federally recognized wine growing areas. There are more than forty wineries scattered through the Leelanau and Old Mission peninsulas. We spent an afternoon on Old Mission touring and tasting. Chateau Grand Traverse offered tastings along a production line. People moved in groups from one station to another—"move along, please." I don't remember the wines, but I do remember the impersonal, industrial style of the place. The best part of this winery: the view of East Bay from its outdoor deck.

By contrast, we enjoyed the wines and tasting style at Bowers Harbor Vineyards. It is smaller—and for me, more appealing than Chateau Grand Traverse. Bowers cultivates twenty acres of vinifera vines, Chateau Grand Traverse about two hundred acres. We were hosted at Bowers by a man who talked interestingly about the white wines. I liked especially the pinot grigio. We also talked about Ohio. Our host had lived in Columbus for many years. I grew up near the city. My father grew up and went to school in the German-speaking South End of Columbus. The host and I shared two interests—wine and place. That made the experience both personal and friendly.

When I first learned there were wineries in northern Michigan, this in the early 1970s, I did have a favorite Leelanau winery—Boskydel. It was the first in the area. Its owner, Bernie Rink, started planting vines in 1965. I liked its white wines, especially its Seyval blanc. And I liked talking with wine pioneer Bernie despite his reputation for being a blunt, curmudgeonly host. He once told a woman who said she liked sweet wines to leave his winery. She wasn't the only one he chased away. Bernie liked tasting his own wines through the day as he talked with customers while his sons ran the business. Boskydel was making three thousand to four thousand cases a year when it closed in 2017 after forty-two years. Bernie died in December 2018 at age ninety-two.

Bernie and his sons operated modestly. The tasting room was small and rudimentary, the parking lot unpaved and small. He did not allow tour buses or caravans. The winery sold only wine—no gifts, souvenirs, or T-shirts. It's as if Bernie resisted the modernization of winemaking by keeping it modest and focused. The family then joined the movement to protect farmland. It placed the farm under a conservation easement with the Leelanau Conservancy. "It was Dad's idea to protect the land," his oldest son said. Besides being a matter of principle, that decision reflected Bernie's independent, cranky personality.

Wine making on the Leelanau and Old Mission peninsulas has grown dramatically since Bernie Rink started Boskydel. The wine trail now includes twenty-four award-winning wineries. The economic impact is significant. The industry is valued at $5.4 billion and has created twenty-eight thousand jobs, according to *Grist*. This industry might well benefit from climate change. Warming temperatures will extend the growing season and make cultivation of, e.g., cabernet sauvignon grapes possible.

• • •

I'd been on the Old Mission Peninsula several times in past years, but not to visit wineries. One summer, I ran on paved roads almost every day for two weeks, up and down hills and dunes, often with a view of the bay. It's the only place I've ever experienced a runner's high—a truly euphoric, almost blissful feeling. Running down a hill, looking at East Bay in the distance, I felt I could leap and land in the water easily. Except for two weeks of running in Chianti, where I ran on country roads, past vineyards, through villages, up and down the Tuscan hills, Old Mission runs satisfied me more than any others.

And then the peninsula's dark side. I've never forgotten the fate of my friends Alice and Elwood Lawrence. Elwood and I were colleagues in the English department at Michigan State. For years, his warmth and wry wit charmed me. I remember Alice as a pleasant and generous woman who smiled every time I met her. I visited them at their Old Mission summer home once. A few years later, fire erupted in the house. Alice escaped. Elwood did not. Alice was never the same.

• • •

We drove a week later to Bay View, where we booked a suite for three nights at the Bay View Inn. In 1875, a group of Michigan Methodists organized a "Camp Meeting" for the "scientific and intellectual culture and the promotion of the Christian religion and morality." They chose Bay View as the site because of "its salubrious summer climate, its beautiful location on the shores of Little Traverse Bay, and its availability by railroad and lake steamer"—the qualities that make the area a major tourist attraction. Lake Michigan and the bay once again captured a community with the lake's beauty and power.

Bay View soon became part of the Chautauqua movement that offered programs of religion, recreation, education, and the performing arts. It rapidly developed from a summer tent community into one of the most interesting Victorian villages in the country. It was established as a summer resort near the lake. It differs noticeably, however, from Traverse City, Harbor Springs, and Harbor Point because of its Methodist and Chautauqua mission.

I have known about Bay View for years—even before I left Ohio and long before I lived in Michigan. But I shared Beth's wonder as we walked through the village admiring the Victorian cottage and house architecture and the colorful ways the buildings have been restored. Bay View is built on bluffs (or dunes) near the end of Little Traverse Bay. It consists of roughly 440 houses—most constructed in the first twenty-five years of the community. Many have a view of the bay, and from those near the top, residents can see the mouth and the big lake beyond. Virtually all are listed on the National Historic Register—as is the entire community. There are also more than thirty public buildings. We enjoyed simply walking there, but music from a single trumpet and then a flute—summer students practicing in one of the public buildings—added a special moment. The community still offers music, film, lecture, and recreation programs throughout the season. There is even a community publication, *Bay View Literary Magazine*.

My own history with Bay View and Little Traverse Bay begins in my hometown. Mrs. Russell, the mother of my parents' close

Bay View house

friends, Bill and Skip Russell, owned a Bay View cottage. I visited there once, but I don't know when or why. I do remember quite clearly, however, that each May, Bill hosted my father and several other men for a long, rowdy weekend of golf and beer. Most of the men drove for twelve hours to get there, but Bill flew his own single-engine airplane. My father served as "Cookie." He prepared the meals for the weekend. He also shared responsibility for playing golf and drinking some of the beer.

As an adult, I've stayed at the Bay View Inn several times. It's a comfortable, Victorian hotel and part of the Bay View community. It stands just steps from the bay. The inn opened in 1886 as the Woodland House, became The Howard House in 1888, then the Bay View Inn in 1935. It has been well maintained and modernized and now is part of the Stafford family restaurant and inn business. Every morning we enjoyed breakfasts (served with an obligatory sweet roll) in the inn's restaurant that gave a view to the flower gardens in full bloom and then across the green lawn to the bay.

I see Beth in one of my photos, standing barefooted at the stony edge of Little Traverse Bay, looking at me and smiling. She is dressed in white leggings, a blue top, and white baseball cap. She's been wading and looking for rare Petoskey stones—fossil stones from Devonian coral that lived 350 million years ago when Michigan was covered by a warm, shallow sea. Although people find the stones across northern Michigan, Little Traverse Bay is the most likely source. The term "Petoskey" comes from a Native American legend and word, *Petosegay,* the name given to a baby, and meaning "rising sun" or "rays of dawn." The nearby modern town of Petoskey was established in the 1870s, shortly before the death of the actual Petosegay, and honors the heritage of "sunbeams of promise."

...

The small resort city of Harbor Springs is located on the north side of Little Traverse Bay. It fronts the deepest harbor on Lake Michigan. Its main street is lined with designer shops, as well as businesses that support the population. Its last census counted almost 1,200 full-time residents. In summer, it grows with people living for a time in their second (or third?) homes—remodeled old structures or striking and expensive contemporary houses. It was raining lightly the afternoon we were there but not hard enough to disrupt the downtown street fair or keep us from walking through nearby neighborhoods. When we drove through residential areas outside the village, the luxury and affluence of the town was apparent. Modern Harbor Springs is far from being Victorian.

During one college summer, I worked as a busboy at the Harbor Point Clubhouse—the inn of the wealthy, gated, residential Harbor Point community. It is part of Harbor Springs, although not easily accessible. I remember the Point as a place of large older houses and the inn as a frame building with a large dining room and guest rooms above the first floor. We worked three meals a day, eating our own in a spartan dining room on the "other side" of the kitchen before we served the guests. We attended to their specific requirements—one woman insisting that a hot cup of coffee land on her table as her bum landed on the chair; another required the coffee to be placed on her table five minutes before she arrived, so that it would be drinkable immediately . . . and so on.

Besides bussing tables in the mornings, I carried a heavy metal "bun box" filled with breakfast rolls and pastries kept warm by a burning charcoal brick in a lower drawer. All went smoothly until one morning, at a table of young couples, I leaned over a woman's shoulder and said my usual, "Would you like a warm roll this morning, madam?" The whole table erupted in laughter. (What might they have been doing before breakfast?) I changed my pitch for the rest of the summer. I also remember spilling fruit cocktail on the table in front of Floyd Alford, the hotel manager. He smiled grimly.

Staff quarters and our dining room were situated next to the inn, facing Little Traverse Bay. We'd walk out the door and across a stretch of grass to get to the waterside. The inn, however, no longer exists. It was razed in 1963—less than ten years after I worked there. The costs of repair and maintenance were exceeding the income the hotel generated. It was old and out of date and not easily accessible. Guests could get to it only by horse and carriage or by boat. The clubhouse had also lost its appeal to the younger generations of the affluent. That was the fate of so many places from our past.

...

That summer I worked on the periphery of the service or support economy. It includes an almost endless list of people—contractors, carpenters, electricians, plumbers, mechanics, service-station attendants, salesclerks, bakers and chefs, food-service staffs, dock workers, small-business owners, and on and on. Their jobs depend on the affluent and the tourists. Unlike Jerry Dennis, who has written so well in "Bending Nails" about his years in the building trades of the area, I have not worked in northern Michigan except for that one summer.

I do remember how able and exacting, and stern, yet generous, the maître d' was at the Harbor Point Clubhouse. He controlled the dining room almost as if it were a military base. And I remember, as well, the impressive baker in the inn's kitchen. Her popovers were wonderful. Every week, she carved a beautiful ice swan as the centerpiece of a weekly Sunday buffet for the guests and Point residents. But to explain further, I turn to my own experience to describe the character, commitment, and skill of many from the support world.

I'm assuming the contractors, carpenters, painters, plumbers, masons, and electricians I worked with building houses resemble those in the building trades there—the people Jerry Dennis writes about. I remember these three most clearly.

Jimmy, a twenty-one-year-old freckle-faced redhead, was married directly out of high school and already was a father. A skilled carpenter, he could also lay block, handle a front loader, and sheet and shingle roofs—he could do almost any job on site. Able and professional as he was, he seemed frustrated, maybe dissatisfied with his personal life—frequently expressing a desire for other women.

I also remember Bob, a composed, courteous, true professional. Like any carpenter, he could build stud walls, nail subflooring, and place joists and rafters. But he revealed the true craft, even artistry, of finish carpentry by hanging doors. They didn't come already fitted into frames. So, Bob first built the frame, added the one-half-inch-by-two-inch pieces the door swung against, then carefully placed the door so that it swung true. He was meticulous.

His brother, Paul, was an equally able carpenter. He dealt with me somewhat sternly, as well as helpfully. One day he was teaching me finish carpentry. I'd cut a piece for the doorframe a half inch short. He looked at it, then at me, looked at it again, then back to me, and said "OK, now what do you do?" Perplexed and embarrassed, I couldn't think. He waited a beat or two, then said, "You cut another one [stupid!]"

By referring to my own experience, I'm simply trying to suggest the skills and value of these professionals in northwest Michigan and elsewhere. I'm omitting, to be sure, significant parts of the area economy (like agriculture), as well as oversimplifying a complex system to make a point. The affluent and tourist worlds differ from the service and support worlds, but they depend on one another. Without the skill and craftsmanship of men like Jimmy, Bob, and Paul—and all those in Michigan who bring to life an owner's or an architect's design—people would have no way of realizing their housing dreams. Most of us couldn't build the houses ourselves. The craftsmen provide the skill, but they also depend on the owners and architects for their living. These different worlds are inextricably intertwined for all their separate identities. They move and flow together yet remain distinct.

• • •

We booked seats on the Shepler ferry from Mackinaw City to Mackinac Island during a 2018 trip. Years before that, when I crossed, I greeted Bill Shepler, one of the owners, before we boarded. He was a fraternity brother at Ohio Wesleyan, two years ahead of me, and played guard on the football team. Knowing I was there, Shep decided to pilot the boat himself. In college and that summer, he was a warm, joyful man who smiled a lot. Before we boarded this time, I asked the ticket window salesperson if Shep was still around. "Yes, but he's retired and no longer comes to the ferry." So, no reunion. The ferry headed west, first toward Mighty Mac, the five-mile bridge across the straits from northern Michigan to the Upper Peninsula, sailed under it, then turned and headed for the island. The view from underneath the long, high bridge made me feel small and vulnerable.

We were heading obviously for the Mackinac Island tourist world—its fudge and T-shirt shops, its galleries and restaurants, inns and hotels, its innumerable horse-drawn carriages and bicycles, and the Grand Hotel. We were also time-traveling into the deep history of Mackinac Island, the Straits of Mackinac, and Lake Michigan.

• • •

The currents at the straits can flow, unpredictably, in every direction—north, south, east, west; they can change within an hour. A boat can be "whipsawed by currents unlike anywhere else on the Great Lakes" (Egan, *Milwaukee Sentinel*). In 1978, I made a very different crossing in a small sailboat that a young professor, Jay Keeley, had towed all the way from Mississippi. He was determined to sail across the straits to the island. We put in at St. Ignace, on the north side of the bridge. At first, the boat sailed smoothly—an easy crossing. But then a huge wave came up behind us and pushed the boat forward and strong currents forced us one way and then another. Jay had never sailed such waters, nor had he looked at any charts or read about the straits. We were in real danger of capsizing or foundering. But caught off guard as he was, Jay did not panic. He recovered, adjusted, and sailed us to safe harbor, but not before many tense and dangerous moments.

. . .

The Shepler ferry made an easy, smooth trip. Once off the boat, we walked and walked, first along the main, touristy street of fudge shops, T-shirts, hats and caps, sandals and flip-flops, pizza, and every other souvenir tourists buy. People get around on foot, bicycle, or horse-drawn carriage. The island allows no cars, not even for residents. We escaped tourist-world as quickly as we could, walked along the East Bluff lined with summer "cottages," then to the Grand Hotel with its splendid 660-foot-long covered front porch and its exceptional view of the straits.

We then looked at several galleries, somewhat away from Main Street, and walked up to Fort Mackinac, where we spent several hours. The fort sits high on a bluff and offers a remarkable view across the straits, then left, far into Lake Huron, and right, to Lake Michigan—the reason for its location. We were greeted by guides, costumed and acting as soldiers and staff from the 1880s. We toured the buildings, viewed artifacts, saw the soldiers' quarters, watched the firing of 1870 Springfield rifles by staff in military uniform, and heard the cannon fired—all the usual tourist things.

The fort dates from the late 18th century. Built in 1780, the Officer's Stone Quarters is the oldest building in Michigan. The rest of the fort's fourteen white limestone buildings were constructed from the 1790s on. All have been restored and have served as a museum since 1959.

For me, the fort and Mackinac Island distill the entire history of the upper lakes and the straits, beginning with the indigenous First People, and forward to the tourists, summer residents, business owners, and employees of the present moment. That history comprehends the military presence and conflicts over two centuries, the cultural changes, and the economic activity, as well—fur trading, fishing, shipping, sailing, tourism—all the business of the upper lakes, from the Native Americans and the French fur trade to the lake freighters which pass through the straits every shipping day.

Paleo-Indians had presumably been living in the Great Lakes basin for ten thousand years. They canoed through the straits and along the lakeshore, fishing and hunting. Archaeologists have found evidence of prehistoric fishing camps on Mackinac Island that date from around 900 AD—seven hundred years before the first white men "discovered" the straits and Lake Michigan. Native Americans had developed a sophisticated culture, organized politically as tribes of the Algonquin nation, and had a long, if unwritten, history. They'd established hunting and fishing communities throughout the Great Lakes, as well as an extensive subsistence agriculture. They lived in villages—dome-shaped, covered lodges in winter and rectangular, bark houses in summer—which they'd move from time to time.

The French arrived early in the 17th century. Samuel de Champlain laid the foundation for New France. By 1615 he had explored as far as Georgian Bay in Lake Huron. Later, the French government sent Jean Nicolet to go further and make peace with the Native Americans. He passed through the Straits of Mackinac into the northern part of Lake Michigan in 1634. Fur traders subsequently moved in and out of the area. The Jesuit priest Claude

Dabon established a mission on Mackinac Island in 1670. Three years later Jacques Marquette moved the mission to St. Ignace—now the city at the north end of Mighty Mac. With the mission as a base, the straits became an important fur trading area for the French. They established a trading post on the mainland in 1715 to support the fur trade and then built Fort Michilimackinac to control the straits.

Nouvelle-France extended from Quebec City and the St. Lawrence west to *Louisiane*—later, the Louisiana purchase. It encompassed all of the Great Lakes, most of the old Northwest Territory, and areas north of Lake Superior. It lasted from 1634 to 1763. The continuing wars between the French and English culminated in the French and Indian War, waged from 1754 to 1763. The French lost and surrendered all of Canada and the upper lakes to the English. New France effectively disappeared—although Quebec sustains that heritage and language. And all of Canada is formally bilingual. That heritage is also visible in Michigan place names—Cadillac, Marquette, Charlevoix, Detroit.

The British moved the fort from the mainland to Mackinac Island, where it would be less vulnerable and provide a better view of the straits. At the end of the Revolutionary War, in 1783, the British ceded the entire straits area to the Americans. During the War of 1812, the British and Americans fought two battles on the island. The British surprised the Americans, who apparently didn't know war had been declared, and captured the fort and the island at the beginning of the war. They built a fort behind and above Fort Mackinac. In 1814, the Americans tried to take back the island but failed. The peace treaty restored the fort, island, straits, and the surrounding area to the Americans. The fort's military purpose ended in the late 19th century. Mackinac Island was designated a national park in 1875. It then developed rapidly as a tourist and summer resident destination.

After lunch at the fort, we headed back to the ferry. Beth liked the return crossing, I think, as much as Mackinac Island—speeding across the water, breaking through modest waves, the wind blowing in our faces, the sun hanging low in the sky. It was her first time on the water where Michigan and Huron meet.

Mackinac Island no longer serves a military or commercial purpose. It has developed well beyond its initial role as a national park into a "destination" for tourists. As a place of history, the island introduces visitors to the story of the upper lakes—if they bother to seek it. The island also suffers from all the excesses of tourist "destinations"—far too many people in search only of the immediate and superficial at famous places. I do enjoy the island, but only if I can escape from the hordes of people that crowd the streets nearest the docks. Even so, I am still, in some sense, one of them—eagerly riding the ferry across the straits to a famous destination. But I also try to think well about all the island has been through over its more than one thousand years of known history.

...

The Bay View Inn and the village, Mackinac Island, the wineries, Traverse City, everything I introduced Beth to in 2018—and all I've written about—exists because of Lake Michigan. The water, the expanse, its many faces still fascinate me—it is magical, even mesmerizing: when it is quiet and resting along the beach under a bright, sun-filled sky, or when waves crash there and sand blows in my face, or when snow and ice build along the shore and the harsh wind chills me. I am captivated by it all. I marvel, as well, at the economic and social activity that goes on *because* of Lake Michigan. The lake enables and produces it all—and in a sense owns it all.

The Grand Traverse economy stands among the top ten Michigan counties in high average income, low unemployment, and the lowest percentage of people living below the poverty line. The northern counties away from the lake average much lower incomes, higher unemployment, and more people living in poverty. The lake makes a difference.

The lake is also an independent natural phenomenon, a power we cannot altogether control. We can write about it or paint and photograph it, but it will always exceed our grasp. We can damage it through pollution and disrupt its natural balances by giving invasive species and organisms entry. We have not yet, however, either controlled or destroyed it—try in a sense as we might. It remains part of the wild for all our hubris. We do, however, continue to benefit from its economic power, and we exploit and damage it to achieve those benefits—like we have done to most of the natural world.

• 13 •

Water 5

"Water, the greatest of desires, is the truly inexhaustible, divine gift."
Gaston Bachelard

We landed in Dubai after dark, so I couldn't see the miles and miles of desert we passed over. We were met and escorted through customs and baggage collection, on through the glittering Dubai terminal—past the gold and luxury shops, and then outside. "Whoa!" The suffocating heat of the desert left me gasping. Our driver took us to the Al Bustan Rotana, a luxury hotel that over time would become a kind of second home. From car to lobby, I felt the smothering heat once again. I walked quickly into the cooling comfort of the hotel lobby and checked in. The next morning, I began to understand the value of water to the Emirati Arabs—especially in the stifling summer heat of the desert.

Dubai and Abu Dhabi have placed pools, fountains, gardens, and grass throughout the cities. The universities I advised built large pools or other water features on their campuses. Upscale restaurants and hotels sprayed fine mists on their outdoor dining areas to keep guests cool but not wet. Pools and fountains enriched the exteriors and lobbies of hotels and professional buildings throughout the cities. It seemed like water, water, everywhere.

Driving along the highway on the outskirts of Dubai, I saw dry, sandy desert extending endlessly on one side and on the other (the city side), grass, flowers, gardens, pools, fountains, and trees. The highway median from Dubai to Al Ain, a desert city, has been planted with greenery and is watered all the way—as is the highway between Dubai and Abu Dhabi. The Emirates' scarce annual rainfall could not provide any of this. Its wealth does. Besides being functionally and aesthetically pleasing—and perhaps extravagant—water also represents an Arab cultural and spiritual need.

∙ ∙ ∙

I have been writing so far about the corporeal, sensory, psychological, and aesthetic appeals and satisfactions of water—in my case of Lake Michigan. I've been writing, as well, about the natural, economic, social, and cultural power of the lake and also about its destructive capacity. I am speaking only for myself.

For humanity broadly, there is much more to think about. We emerge as beings from months in amniotic fluid. Water constitutes 60 percent of our corporeality. We cannot survive without water for drinking. We must have rain for growing crops. We depend on ponds, streams, rivers, lakes, and the ocean for food. We use water for cleansing, bathing, pleasure. We depend on water for transportation. We value waterfront property as more desirable and valuable than inland places. We build cities around it. We cannot live without water.

The water-based rituals and practices of virtually every culture and religion give still greater significance and power to water. It brings serenity and calmness; it purifies and transforms; it is the source of wisdom or the path to enlightenment. It symbolizes birth, fertility, life, and cleansing.

In Native American cultures, breath, wind, and water connect all things. Water has a cleansing, purifying power and can represent strength, healing, dreaming. Water is sacred. The Odawas, e.g., the Grand Traverse Bay and Little Traverse Bay Bands, were (and are) deeply connected to nature. They relied on the lake for fishing and movement to hunting grounds. They used the lake for trade and transport, navigating the tricky waters with great skill, especially the difficult currents in the straits and the crossing of Grand Traverse

Bay. They established villages close to the lake. They buried their dead near water. Spirits dwelled in water. Their creation spirit, Gitchie Manitou, dwells on Mackinac Island. Water functioned in every part of their lives, from sustenance to spirituality. The tribes continue to interact ceremonially with water and are deeply engaged in water resource issues.

Christianity, Hinduism, and Buddhism all believe that water cleanses or purifies in some way. "Blessed water" is used in most Buddhist traditions. In Hinduism, water represents God in a spiritual sense. In my cultural tradition, we are baptized with water. Baptism is the first of the two great sacraments in the Episcopal Church. It is a sign of cleansing and of ritual death and rebirth in Jesus Christ, as well. "Holy" water is used for blessing people—a sign of renewed baptism and a prayer for protection. And sometimes water is mixed with wine in the chalice for the Eucharist—the other great sacrament. Mixing suggests the joining of the human and the divine.

Water is fundamental in Islam. "The Quran describes the life-giving properties of water by referring to the clouds that bring rains, irrigate lands, bring back the barren farm to life . . . Water is described to be the greatest bounty from God" (Siraj and Tayab). Muslims need water for survival, especially in desert climates. Historically, they searched constantly for water sources. Water also serves as a social good in their tradition of hospitality; Muslims make gifts of water to strangers; water is a blessing from Allah and sustains all life; and truly devout Muslims wash ritually before prayer—five times a day. The Koran says, "God created every moving thing from water" (Ali, 302). Water possesses no sanctity but is necessary and fundamental—sacred at least in practical and cultural senses. The Emirati uses of water might seem lavish, even wasteful, but water expresses a deep cultural and spiritual value.

...

In *Blue Mind*, Wallace Nichols cites many neurological, psychological, and sociological studies that show our Blue Mind is "real"—that "being near water makes us healthier, happier, reduces stress, and brings us peace" (11). We might even be hardwired for Blue Mind. In the last part of his book, Nichols reaches beyond the secular and scientific. "Something mystical" can happen when we're close to nature, especially to water. "Water's infinite variety and (sometimes terrifying) depth has an unrivaled inspirational force when it comes to the physical world. Its potential is metaphysical to the nth degree" (183, 195). Grounded in material and mental worlds, and in science, *Blue Mind* then gestures toward the metaphysical—and perhaps the sacred and spiritual—meanings of water. Nichols asks us, in the end, to live our Blue Minds and "stay connected with all of the many, many blessings that water provides" (268).

He does acknowledge the ambiguity of the word "blue." It sometimes suggests melancholy or sadness, coldness, sorrow, even death—the "dark side" of the word that singing the blues expresses. The blues might console, perhaps calm, by singing about melancholy, suffering, and loss—momentarily releasing musicians and listeners from their "blues"—but as for making people healthier, happier, less stressed, peaceful? I'm not sure. The dark side persists. But in the end, Nichols insists on blue's powerful and positive qualities. "Fall more deeply in love with water in all its shapes, colors, and forms. Let it heal you and make you a better, stronger version of yourself. You need water. And water needs you now" (276).

• • •

But there's still another turn. The blue-mind impulse to be near water can lead to high-risk, destructive, and costly consequences. That is, people rebuild houses in flood plains—sometimes repeatedly. They might not be able to afford other property, but the desire to be near water figures as well. The affluent build more and more expensive homes, in greater and greater density, along coasts and lakeshores. They build on land at serious risk for flooding from high lake water or rising sea levels or from damage or destruction from hurricanes—or even storms on the Great Lakes.

Florida is a perfect example of the risk and cost of being near water. It "is uniquely vulnerable. More than $1 trillion worth of property straddles the coast," including a million properties in a "special flood hazard area." Zillow has estimated that "rising seas [alone] could swallow upward of a million Florida homes." That doesn't even account for hurricanes (Gaul, 114).

FEMA now covers 70 percent of disaster relief costs—at billions and billions of dollars. A personal loss, but a federal cost. "It results in a big income transfer from the poor to the rich" (Gaul, 107). There is a financial incentive, in effect, to take on greater and greater risk. Couple that with the blue-mind desire for water, and the impulse becomes even stronger. It is not just Florida, but every coastal city that faces similar risks.

When the sun shines, the temperatures rise, and water does not. Beach and coastal living can provide a healthier, happier, less stressful, and more peaceful way of life. But when water and wind do rise and damage and destroy, stress, confusion, and anger follow. Like everything else about water and Lake Michigan, I am left with ambiguities.

• 14 •

The Force of the Lake

"The imagined fact is more important than the real fact."
Gaston Bachelard

Some places possess a natural power—like hometowns—that ground us and shape us in fundamental ways. We do not choose these primal places, but instead we're born into them. We are embedded in them. Our identities are formed substantially by them.

For those of us who have lived in multiple places and for prolonged periods, there are locations like Clover Hollow that become significant because we make them so—because we need a sense of place, of belonging. They might become sites of discovery and thereby primary places in our histories—as Clover Hollow was for me. But we come upon them and make them into what we need. We are not born into them. We draw out their meanings for ourselves and simultaneously create how they influence us.

Sometimes, we force an order, coherence, or meaning on locations that can't bear the burden of the significance or influence we impose on them: places where we have no history and little knowledge, only episodic experiences, and little acquaintance with people. We seize on these as far more meaningful than they are or can be. It makes for a good story or a moving aesthetic experience. I tried, but I couldn't even do this for Florida.

What then is Lake Michigan for me? It is not really a place in any of these senses, no matter how important it seems to be. It is rather a presence which gathers diverse, occasional, episodic experiences—at different times of my life—into a single force that constitutes my lifelong fascination with the lake. It is a presence in its very absence—mostly out there, up there, but alive within me.

Along the lake, people transform open beach into meaningful places by building homes. Others build docks at the edge of the lake for boats they sail and sometimes live on, thereby creating a kind of moveable place on the lake. Scientists have managed the lake's fishery to some extent and also have controlled, again to some extent, the destructive invasions of non-native fish, mollusks, and organisms. Ships navigate the lake's waters. People sail on it, swim in it, and gaze at it, but no human activity takes it over and quite transforms it into a place of human habitation. It remains a natural force that functions beyond our control—as the high and low water rhythms or the storms that sink ships suggest. The lake is itself, although not what it once was. And it remains a presence for me, although it's no longer the lake of my childhood.

• • •

I am writing about Lake Michigan specifically and about water generally—but only insofar as that helps me understand the lake-out-there and the lake-in-me. I sense the powerful presence of the lake when I am there. My feelings range from simple satisfactions to tears. I am moved by its absence and my loss when I'm away. Even then, however, Lake Michigan is present in its absence—present in my memory and imagination and in these words I'm writing in my study in the Virginia mountains.

Lake Michigan gathers all the possible material, environmental, personal, social, economic, cultural, and spiritual functions and meanings of water. In that sense it is metaphoric or symbolic, but for me it is far more. The lake is a particular location and a natural presence. I value every moment I'm near it for physical and aesthetic pleasure and psychic satisfactions. I treasure my history with it. A cherished memory, a place to visit, a lake to study—that is the lake-out-there. The lake-in-me holds the real value. My experience with that inward lake reveals so much about life—the pleasure and satisfactions of simply being in the world, the value of memory, the importance of history and understanding contemporary complexity, awareness of the way nature can drive an economy and create a culture, a sense of the sacred in the world, the rhythms of presence and absence and ultimate loss, the force of desire.

•••

In the end, besides being a powerful presence, Lake Michigan is a great *force*. As a natural phenomenon, it asserts power through, let's say, the two magics I've suggested. We try to manage this natural force, but so far, we have neither controlled nor dominated it. We have compromised and damaged the lake, and one day we might destroy it, along with our planet. But so far, Lake Michigan persists as a beautiful and powerful force of nature.

The lake is also a potent force in the lives of people. It enables and sustains an economy. The lake "owns" the economy and society of Michigan counties like Leelanau, Grand Traverse, Antrim, Charlevoix, and Emmet. Fishing, boating, tourism, summer residents, the cherry industry, and viniculture enabled by the lake-effect climate—all drive those economies and have created a water-oriented society and culture along and near the lake.

These abstractions, however—aesthetic, psychic, economic, social, cultural—are inseparably intertwined in our lives. We live them *in situ*. They might help us understand Lake Michigan, but they do not express or tell anyone's story, or my story of the lake-in-me.

•••

I remain transfixed by Lake Michigan, and like one of Melville's people, I seek water and the lake. I must get as "nigh" to it as I possibly can. When I give myself entirely to this wonder and set aside all that I know about it, all the ways it has been compromised and threatened, it takes me out of myself into a momentary timelessness—into a different consciousness, as my Earth-turn moment did. For some people, these might even be sacred moments in harmony with a lake that itself is sacred. I'm, however, too time-bound and secular to presume that for myself. Yet as metaphor, as a way of identifying something special—a transcendent, selfless experience—"sacred" might be right.

• 15 •

Leaving Lake Michigan

We were driving away from Little Traverse Bay, following the highway up a hill and out of Bay View. Behind us, reflected in the rearview mirror, I could see the bay and far out its mouth Lake Michigan. We were leaving, and I wondered if I'd ever see "my" great lake, again. Memories of Lake Michigan flashed by as the road, lined by northern Michigan woods, opened to take us away. The bay disappeared, but I visualized, one more time, walks across the sand dunes, my parents and relatives lying on blankets at the beach, the scattering of houses facing the lake, the waves breaking on the shore—then in later decades, summers and winters along the lake, warm sun, calm water, blinding snow, ice mountains, hikes through the dunes in sun and shade, then looking out over the lake from a four-hundred-foot dune, delighting in Beth's wonder as she discovered Lake Michigan for the first time and learned why it has so captivated me. The memories and images flowed on and on as we drove further and further away. Time and age might let us come back but also might not. So many departures are now true farewells—people never to see again, places never to visit. This might be the end of the lake for me—I couldn't help but think and fear. So, I write. I look at the beach paintings from my grandparents' house. I study my South Shore posters. I remember. I long. And I wonder.

Fred on a Lake Michigan beach

ACKNOWLEDGMENTS

Once again, I have benefitted enormously from the readings by and advice from my constant and tireless readers—Beth Obenshain, Jana Carlisle, Bob Siegle, Edward Weisband, and Tom Gardner. I appreciate the readings at various stages by Lindy Carlisle Martin, Ginna Lee Quintanilla, Becky Newman, Blaine Brownell, Lloyd Gardner, and Ralph Byers. I appreciate, as well, the wonderful appraisals of my book by Anne-Marie Oomen, Nancy Grayson, Tom Gardner, and William Rapai. The Mission Point Press team led by Tanya Muzumdar has been remarkably helpful and pleasant to work with. I am impressed by their talent, experience and professionalism—to Tanya, especially, to Sarah Meiers for a beautiful design, to Hart Cauchy for proofreading, to Tricia Frey for valuable guidance on marketing, and to Noah Shaw for my fine, new web site. Sommer Poquette and Maddie Shelton of Keep It Real Social have been helpful, as well. I am grateful, as well, to Doug Weaver of Mission Point Press. He has been warm and encouraging from our first contact. I also appreciate the assistance on specifics by Sarah (Pippi) Miller of Miller off Main St. Galleries in Blacksburg, VA; Jennifer Wcisel of the Grand Rapids Art Museum; Mike Gillis of MLive; Colleen Layton, rights and reproductions coordinator at the Chicago History Museum; and William Rapai, executive director of the Kirtland's Warbler Alliance and author of *Lake Invaders*, for his image of a sea lamprey. I am especially grateful to Alexis Rockman for permission to use his remarkable painting, "Cascade," for the cover of this book.

NOTES AND SOURCES

1. Origins: Ogden Dunes
Bachelard, Gaston. *Water and Dreams*. The Dallas Institute for Humanities and Culture, 1982, 176.
Cohen, Ronald and Stephen G. McShane, editors. *Moonlight in Duneland: The Illustrated Story of the Chicago South Shore and South Bend Railroad*. Indiana UP, 1998.
Grady, Wayne. *The Great Lakes: The Natural History of a Changing Region*. Vancouver, Greystone Books, 2007.
Meister, Dick, Ken Martin, and the Historical Society of Ogden Dunes. *Ogden Dunes, Images of America*. Charleston, SC, 2014.
Ogden Dunes Historical Society. www.odhistory.org/history-of-ogden-dunes.
Schoon, Kenneth J. *Dreams of Duneland: A Pictorial History*. Indiana UP, 2013.
Town of Ogden Dunes, Indiana. www.ogdendunes.in.gov/about-ogden-dunes.

2. Origins: The Lucas Home in Gary, Indiana
All That's Interesting. www.allthatsinteresting.com/gary-indiana). About the mayor of Gary.
Davich, Jerry. *Lost Gary Indiana*. Charleston, SC, The History Press, 2015.
"Gary Works." *Wikipedia*.
Glass, James. "When Gary, Indiana, Was a Model City." *Indianapolis Star*, March 2, 2018.
Quaife, Milo. *Lake Michigan. The American Lakes Series*. Bobbs-Merrill, 1944.
St. Mary's Mercy Hospital. www.sometimes-interesting.com/2013/06/30/abandoned-st-marys-mercy-hospital/.
Young, David. "Gary Works Made of Steel." *Chicago Tribune*, February 26, 1996.

Information about Bob Elson, Jack Brickhouse, the Chicago Cubs, and the Chicago White Sox came from various internet sites.

Information about the Chicago Elevated came from various internet sources.

Family manuscript histories.

3. Water I

Epigraph: Bachelard, 8.

Melville, Herman. *Melville: Redburn, White Jacket, Moby-Dick*. The Library of America, 796.

Melville, Herman. *Melville, Typee, Omoo, Mardi*. The Library of America, 11.

Nichols, Wallace. *Blue Mind*. New York, Little, Brown Spark, 2014.

4. Rediscovering Lake Michigan

Epigraph: Nichols. "I wish you water," 276.

Egan, Dan. *The Death and Life of the Great Lakes*. New York, W.W. Norton, 2017.

Lavey, Kathleen. "What's the Future for Great Lakes Salmon?" *Lansing State Journal*, June 6, 2016.

5. Lake Michigan Rising

Epigraph: Gronewold and Rood.

ABC News. May 10, 2021.

Friends of Sleeping Bear Dunes, www.friendsofsleepingbear.org/area-history-articles/manitou-island-history/.

"Glen Haven." *Wikipedia*, www.wikipedia.org/wiki/Glen_Haven

"Glen Haven, Michigan." *Leelanau.com*, www.leelanau.com, March 30, 2008.

Greene, Morgan. "Michigan Beach Town Battles Erosion . . ." *Chicago Tribune*, March 8, 2020.

Gronewold, Drew and Richard B. Rood. "Climate Change Is Driving Rapid Shifts Between High and Low Water Levels on the Great Lakes." *The Conversation*, www.theconversation.com, June 4, 2019.

Hillman-Rapley, Lynda. "Walking on shelf ice can be deadly." *Exeter Lake Shore Advance*, February 3, 2017.

House, Kelly. "Great Lakes." *Bridge Michigan*, July 17, 2020.

Krupa, Greg. "Crumbling Great Lakes Shorelines Have Residents Moving Homes to Safety." *The Detroit News*, January 22, 2020.

Matheny, Keith. "Record-High Michigan Water Levels Are a Nightmare for Home Owners." *Detroit Free Press*, July 17, 2020.

Nissan, Jack. "Great Lakes Water Levels Falling Fast in Lakes Michigan and Huron." Fox 2 Detroit, April 5, 2022.

"North Manitou Island." *Wikipedia*, last edited August 13, 2021.

Purifoy, Stephanie. "Exploring the History of Glen Haven." *MyNorth.com*, July 28, 2016.

Serba, John. "Michigan's Beautiful Manitou Islands in One Succinct (and Silly) Guide." *MLive*, September 19, 2019.

Sleeping Bear Inn. www.sleepingbearinn.org. Multiple news stories about the leasing and potential restoration.

Smith, Mitch. "Summer on the Swollen Great Lakes." *The New York Times*, August 24, 2019.

"The Manitou Islands." *Leland.com*.

Smith, Mitch. "Summer on the Swollen Great Lakes." *The New York Times*, August 24, 2019.

Travis, Jordan. "Lake Michigan's Dropping Levels Pause for Now." *The Traverse City Record-Eagle*, February 18, 2022.

Witkos, Matt. "Great Lakes Water Levels Are 2 Feet Lower Than Records Set in 2020." Fox 17 Western Michigan, February 16, 2022.

6. Water II. Words and Images

Epigraph: *The Living Great Lakes*, 9.

Bachelard, Gaston. "Water's Voice," *Water and Dreams*. The Dallas Institute of Humanities and Culture, 1983.

Dennis, Jerry. *The Living Great Lakes*. New York, St. Martin's Press, 2003.

Dennis, Jerry. *The Windward Shore*. Ann Arbor, University of Michigan Press, 2012.

Friis-Hansen, Dana. *Alexis Rockman, The Great Lakes Cycle*. Grand Rapids Art Museum and Michigan State UP, 2018.

7. The Invasive Juggernaut

Egan, Dan. *The Death and Life of the Great Lakes*.

Invaders of the Great Lakes. Cambridge, MN, Adventure Publications, 2017.

Rapai, William. *Lake Invaders: Invasive Species and the Battle for the Future of the Great Lakes*. Wayne State UP, 2016.

"Sea Lamprey." Great Lakes Fishery Commission, www.glfc.org/sea-lamprey.php.

"Study: Asian Carp Could Find Plenty of Food in Lake Michigan." *AP News*, August 12, 2019.

8. Water 3

Epigraph: Miller, Candice. *Lansing State Journal*. Rpt. in Egan. *The Death and Life*.

Kolbert, Elizabeth. *Under a White Sky: The Nature of the Future*. New York, Crown, 2021.

Rapai, William. *Lake Invaders*.

9. The Return

Epigraph: Stier, May. *Meet Mae Stier*, www.katherinecorden.com/blog/maestier.

10. The Lake Effect

Epigraph: Roethke, Theodore. "Meditation at Oyster River." *The Collected Poems of Theodore Roethke*. Doubleday, 1965, 191.

11. Water 4

Epigraph: Matt Stofsky, "8 Famous Shipwrecks on Lake Michigan." *Mental Floss*, Aug. 17, 2006, www.mentalfloss.com/article/83964/8-famous-shipwrecks-lake-michigan.

"Fix the Soo Locks." *Michigan.gov*, www.michigan.gov/fixthesoolocks.

"Freighter Carl D. Bradley." *Shipwreck Explorers*, www.shipwreckexplorers.

Great Lakes Shipwreck Museum. Display case. Whitefish Point, Michigan.

Mack. "Ranking 16 of Michigan's Great Lake Harbor Communities by Economic Impact." *Mlive*, Published: Apr. 25, 2019, 9:00 a.m. Updated: Sep. 19, 2019, 4:21 p.m.

"Michigan Limestone and Chemical Company." *Wikipedia*, last edited February 1, 2022.

World Port Source, www.worldportsource.com.

"Report: U.S., Michigan Face Dire Consequences if Soo Locks Fail." *The Detroit Free Press*, March 3, 2016.

"SS Carl D. Bradley." *Wikipedia*, last edited February 21, 2022.

Stofsky, Matt. "8 Famous Shipwrecks on Lake Michigan." *Mental Floss*, August 17, 2016, www.mentalfloss.com/article/83964/8-famous-shipwrecks-lake-michigan.

"The Carl D. Bradley Split in Two . . ." *Mlive.com*, November 17, 2019.

"Why the Soo Locks Are So Important to our U.S. Economy." KSAT, March 29, 2021.

12. The Gold Coast: Tourism, Affluence, and the Rest

Egan, Dan. "Dangerous Straits." *Milwaukee Journal Sentinel*, January 18, 2017.

Gaul, Gilbert M. T*he Geography of Risk: Epic Storms, Rising Seas, and the Cost of America's Coasts*. New York, Farrar, Straus and Giroux, 2019.

Grady, Wayne. *The Great Lakes: The Natural History of a Changing Region*. Vancouver, Greystone Books, 2007.

13. Water 5

Epigraph: Bachelard. 148.

Ali, Ahmed. *Al-Qur'ān: A Contemporary Translation.* "The Light," 24: 45.

Gaul, Gilbert M. *The Geography of Risk: Epic Storms, Rising Seas, and the Cost of America's Coasts.*

New York, Farrar, Straus and Giroux, 2019.

Native American sources: See 12: "The Gold Coast: Tourism, Affluence, and the Rest."

Siraj, M.A. and M.A.K. Tayab. Abstract for "Water in Islam." *Water and Scriptures,* May 6, 2017.

"The Importance of Water in Different Cultures." *Zipwater.com.*

"Water in Religions." *Water Encyclopedia,* www.waterencyclopedia.com/Po-Re/Religions-Water-in.html.

14. The Force of the Lake
Epigraph: Bachelard. 177.

SOURCES FOR TOPICS IN THE "GOLD COAST"

Bayview:
> Bay View Association, www.bayviewassociation.org.
> Stafford's Bay View Inn, www.thebayviewinn.com.

Cherry Industry and Festival:
> "Michigan's Cherry Farmers Worry as Cherry Crops Continue to Decline." *Upnorthlive.com*, June 24, 2021.
> "Michigan Tart Cherry Farmers Consider Ways to Survive After Tariffs Revoked." *Interlochenpublicradio.org*, January 30, 2021.
> Michigan's Tart Cherry Growers Blame Weather for Yet Another Low Harvest." *Bridge Michigan*, www.bridgemi.com.
> "National Cherry Festival," *Traverse city.com*, www.cherryfestival.org/p/get-cherries/history-of-cherries.
> Unofficial National Cherry Homepage. *Leelanau.com*, www.leelanau.com/cherry/industry.
> "What You Need to Know About the National Cherry Festival." *UpNorthLive*, July 7, 2021.

Grand Traverse Regional Land Conservancy. www.gtrlc.org/milestone-publications/love-the-land-pass-it-on-the-story-of-the-campaign-for-generations/.

Harbor Springs Historical Society.

"History." The Village at Grand Traverse Commons. www.thevillagetc.com/history/.

Mackinac Island:
> "Chicago and Western Michigan Railway." *Wikipedia*, last edited December 16, 2021.

City of Traverse steamer: www.traversehistory.org/history/timeline/.

Egan, Dan. "Dangerous Straits: A Journal Sentinel Special Report." *Milwaukee Journal Sentinel,* January 18, 2017.

"French Explorers." Michigan State University, www.project.geo.mus.edu.

"Grand Rapids and Indiana Railroad." *Wikipedia,* last edited January 18, 2022.

"Great Lakes Passenger Steamers." *Wikipedia,* last edited October 26, 2021.

"Mackinac Island." *Wikipedia,* last revised February 22, 2022.

Native Americans:

Duran, Betty E.S. "American Indian Belief Systems and Traditional Practices." *Tribal Healing to Wellness Courts,* April 11, 2002, www.wellnesscourts.org › files › Duran - Am….

"Gitche Manitou." *Wikipedia.*

"Native Americans in the Great Lakes Region." Michigan State University, www.project.geo.msu.edu/geomich/paleo-indian.

Nibish Naagdowen, www.nibiishnaagdowen.com/our-water/.

Petoskey Stones:

"Petoskey Stone." *Wikipedia.*

"The Petoskey Stone." Michigan State University, www.project.geo.msu.edu/geogmich/petoskeystone.

Real Estate:

Brown, Yarrow. "Short Term Rentals Affect Year-Round Housing." *Traverse City Record-Eagle,* May 26, 2021.

Nielsen, Dan. "Newsmaker: Housing Market Continues to Astound." *Traverse City Record-Eagle*, December 26, 2021.

"Northern Michigan Real Estate Boom." *Capital News Service*, October 16, 2020.

O'Hara, Robert. "How Can We Fill the Housing Gap?" *Traverse City Record-Eagle*, November 1, 2021.

Sleeping Bear National Lakeshore:

Leelanau.com, www.leelanau.com/dunes/sleeping-bear-history/.

National Park Service, www.nps.gov/parkhistory/online_books/slbe/adhi_2h.htm.

National Park Service, www.nps.gov/slbe/learn/nature/environmentalfactors.htm.

"Sleeping Bear Dunes National Lakeshore." *Wikipedia,* last edited February 18, 2022.

Traverse City State Hospital:

Traverse City State Hospital, "History." www.thevillagetc.com/history/.

"Traverse City State Hospital." *Wikipedia.*

Wine Industry:

"Bernie Rink's Boskydel Vineyard Lands Protected." Leelanau Conservancy, May 7, 2020.

"Oldest Winery on the Leelanau Peninsula Closes Down." *The Detroit News*, December 29, 2017.

"Rising Temperatures Could Make Michigan the Next Great Wine Hub." *Grist.org*, May 12, 2021.

Several other internet sites.

ABOUT THE AUTHOR

Fred Carlisle lived in Michigan for twenty years, raising a young family and teaching at Michigan State University. He enjoyed a long academic career as a professor of English, mainly at Michigan State, and then as a university provost at Miami University in Ohio and then at Virginia Tech in Blacksburg, Virginia.

His fascination with Lake Michigan began when he was just two. An old photograph shows two-year-old "Freddie" on a Lake Michigan beach, ankle deep in the water.

Carlisle grew up in Ohio, and has also lived in Florida and rural Virginia. He now lives with his wife, Beth, on her family farm in the Virginia mountains.

Carlisle has written literary criticism—studies of Walt Whitman and Loren Eiseley—and three memoirs. His most recent book is *Hollow and Home: A Story of Self and Place*.

www.ingramcontent.com/pod-product-compliance
Lightning Source LLC
Chambersburg PA
CBHW020248010526
44107CB00002B/158